Bliss

The Smart Girl's Guide to SEX

Kerry Parnell

Piccadilly Press • London

First published in Great Britain in 2000
by Piccadilly Press Ltd.,
5 Castle Road, London NW1 8PR

Phototypeset from author's disc
in 10.5 pt Futura Book

A catalogue record for this book is available from the
British Library

ISBN: 1 85340 681 3 (paperback)

1 3 5 7 9 10 8 6 4 2

Printed and bound by Creative Print and Design (Wales),
Ebbw Vale

Design & cover design by Judith Robertson

CONTENTS

Chapter 1

PUBERTY

Puberty has to be the silliest name for the weirdest time of your life. When the human-biologist person labelled the time you turn from a child to an adult, why did they have to put the word 'pube' in it? Their legacy is that every year millions of teenage boys nearly give themselves hernias sniggering over it in Sex Ed. Hmm. The comedy name doesn't do credit to the bizarre experience of puberty.

The dictionary definition is the 'stage at which a person becomes capable of procreation through the natural development of the reproductive organs,' but to you and me, it's the time that you start getting boobs, periods, body hair and zits. You start having strange feelings for boys, and your emotions act like they've gone on holiday with a rollercoaster convention. Oh, and your catch-phrase becomes, 'No one understands me!' – cue running off to your room in tears to stare out of the window while playing CDs with meaningful lyrics.

The good news is – everyone goes through it (even she of the perfect marks/perfect skin at school), and you *do* get over it. The even better news is, this chapter's going to show you that boys get it even worse than we do. Basically, it all comes down to one thing – your body is turning into a woman's, and his body is turning into a man's. The rate it happens varies from person to person but, and this is where you can be oh-so superior again, girls usually hit puberty first, which gives us all immense pleasure as we watch the boys getting Bart Simpson squeaky voices and bum fluff on their chins.

HIS BODY

Here's a brief guide to what happens to boys during puberty:

Willy His penis and scrotum (balls) get bigger. He'll start to get hard-ons, often by accident. He'll start to get wet dreams, which are dreams that give him orgasms in the middle of the night.

Body hair He'll get pubic hair, and hair under his armpits. He may get chest and even back hair (though some men never do).

Facial hair The first place he'll get facial hair is on his upper lip. Some boys quickly get a full beard, some never do. He'll have to face up to the fact that he'll have to start shaving, eventually every day.

Skin and hair His hair may get greasier, and he'll have to wash it more often. Plus his skin may become greasy and most boys get plenty of spots.

Sweat Boys start to sweat more, and the smell will be stronger, so at puberty they have to start using deodorant. You'll notice they sometimes use way too much!

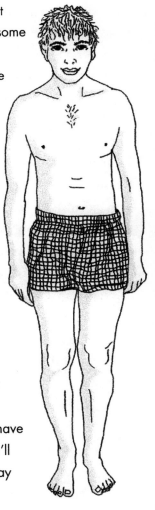

Voice Boys' voices 'break' during puberty, becoming deeper and lower. Some break instantly, some take a long time, hence squeaky voices and wobbly sounds.

Growth He will grow taller, get stronger and put on weight, gradually filling out into a more manly shape.

His Bits

As you read on through this book, you'll be aware that there's loads of misinformation about willies – from old wives' tales, to tall tales boys will spin you to give them a bit of action. So get sussed with our no-nonsense guide to his private parts:

A boy's sexual organs are made up of a penis, testicles and scrotum. He has two testicles (balls), which

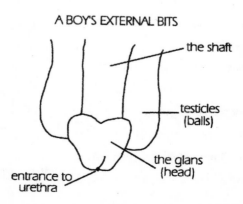

A BOY'S EXTERNAL BITS

the shaft

testicles (balls)

the glans (head)

entrance to urethra

A BOY'S INTERNAL BITS

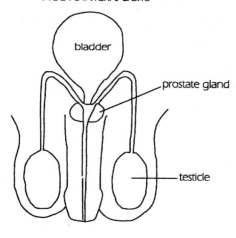

are stored in a sort of bag of skin called the scrotal sac. These contain literally millions of sperm. When he's warm, the balls hang down, but if he gets cold or sexually excited, the balls get firmer, pull themselves up towards the body and appear crinkly. The penis is made of body tissue, full of blood vessels. When he gets excited, blood pumps into the vessels and the willy becomes erect (stands up on its own – i.e. a hard-on) – ready to have sex. The willy itself is made up of a shaft and head, and the head has loads of nerve-endings in it which make it really sensitive. The head is covered by a bit of skin called the foreskin, but if he has been circumcised (for medical

9

or religious reasons), this will have been removed. At the tip of the head is a small opening, which is the end of a tube called the urethra, which is where he wees and ejaculates (see below).

You should note that all boys' willies are different. Some may curve to one side, be bent in the middle, be short and fat, long and thin, whatever. Boys will be forever hung-up on whether their willies are big enough, but you should know that whatever the size they are when they are flaccid, when they are erect they all end up virtually the same – the average erect size is six inches (or fifteen and a half centimetres!).

His orgasm

When a boy gets turned on he develops a hard-on, and if he's having sex or playing with himself, he'll reach a point where he gets a huge rush of excitement, which is when he'll have an orgasm, and ejaculate. What happens here is that semen (whitish fluid that carries sperm) shoots out of the end of his willy, and either makes a mess somewhere or, if he is having sex, goes inside you. Every time he has an orgasm he can ejaculate up to six hundred million sperm in one go, and as just one sperm can make you pregnant, that's why you need to use contraception.

YOUR BODY

Here's a brief guide to what happens to you during
puberty:

Boobs Your nipples get
bigger, sometimes darker and more
sensitive. You develop breasts – the
size and shape depends on your
genes.

Body hair You get pubic
hair, and hair under your armpits. You will also get darker
and thicker hair on your legs.
Most girls shave off armpit
hair, but it's up to you. And
if you don't like your leg hair,
you can shave, wax, or use
depilatory creams to get rid of it.
You may get stray hairs sprouting
up in odd places too – like around
your nipples, on your chin or on
your tummy.

Sweat Like boys, you'll start to
sweat more now, so it's a good idea
to use deodorants and wash regularly.

11

Shape You will put on weight, get stronger, grow taller, and your body will change shape, becoming more curvy, with a smaller waist and bigger hips.

Voice Believe it or not, your voice will get deeper, but you don't usually notice.

Skin and hair Your skin and hair may get greasier, so you'll have to wash your hair more often, and sorry, but you'll be more prone to spots.

Vagina The lips round your vagina will get fuller, and you'll notice some white discharge in your pants, which is perfectly normal. You'll also start your periods.

Your Bits

Girls' sexual organs are nearly all internal, so there's less to see! It sounds very hippy-dippy, but it is worth sitting in front of a mirror to have a look at what's down there – it's your body, so don't be embarrassed. It's important to know that every girl is different, so don't worry that the size and shape of your genitals may be different to everyone else's!

External

Vagina This is the passage that lets a penis in during sex, and lets your periods out. It's also where the baby comes out from your womb.

Hymen You may still have a hymen, which is a thin piece of skin covering the entrance to the vagina, but many girls' hymens break through sport or vigorous activity long before they lose their virginity.

Labia These are the lips round your vagina. There is a small set close to the vagina, and then a larger outer set.

Urethra Contrary to what you might think, your wee doesn't come out of your vagina, it comes out of this tiny hole, which is the end of a tube that leads to your bladder.

A GIRL'S EXTERNAL BITS

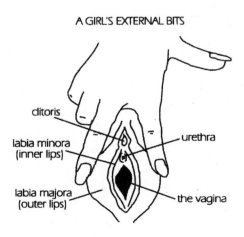

clitoris

labia minora
(inner lips)

labia majora
(outer lips)

urethra

the vagina

13

Clitoris This is a little bump of tissue, protected by a hood of skin, that makes you feel excited when touched sexually. It's a bit like a willy in that it has blood vessels in it which, when you are turned on, receive increased blood flow, making it go hard and bigger (the change is not noticeable). Stimulation of the clitoris will often lead to orgasm.

Internal

Cervix This is the entrance to the womb, and is a tiny hole at the top of the vagina. It's too small for

A GIRL'S INTERNAL BITS

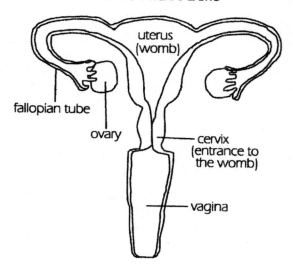

fallopian tube

uterus (womb)

ovary

cervix (entrance to the womb)

vagina

anything to go into it, so don't worry about losing tampons or even willies up there!

Ovaries These are two oval-shaped structures that hold your eggs (for baby-making).

Fallopian tubes These are thin tubes that carry the egg from the ovaries to the uterus (womb) every month, ready to be fertilised.

Uterus This is the womb, which prepares itself every month to receive the egg if it has been fertilised (by sperm). When this doesn't happen, the womb sheds its thick wall lining – this is your period.

Your orgasm

Unlike boys, when girls have an orgasm they do not ejaculate anything. Moisture in the vagina increases, but there aren't any other physical signs that you've had an orgasm. You will feel a rush of excitement/ sensation, which then reaches a crescendo, making you sort of shudder. That's your orgasm.

Chapter 2

PERIODS

The big change to your body through puberty is getting your period – and then realising you're going to get it every month for about another thirty-five years!

Girls start their periods at different ages – from as early as eight, to as late as eighteen. Don't worry if your mate gets hers before you, everyone's different. Even your actual periods are different – they can last from two days to eight, and can be on a cycle of anything from every twenty-one days to thirty-five (the average is twenty-eight).

What's happening to you

One of your ovaries releases a ripe egg and sends it down your Fallopian tube to your womb. Your womb has built up a thick lining so that if the egg is ferti-lised by sperm it will embed itself in the thick lining and grow, to become a baby. When it isn't fertilised, the body gets rid of everything – the egg and the lining, which comes out as blood and contains tiny bits of tissue. That's your period. The whole process is called your menstruation cycle. As I said, it's an average of twenty-eight days long. You start counting from the first day of your period. Ovulation is mid-way through your cycle. You know when you are about to start your period as you will probably get cramping and a small amount of spotting of blood in your pants. Don't worry, it doesn't come gushing out, and you actually only lose a small amount of blood each period (it's about four–six tablespoons) – it just seems like a lot.

Period pain

Unfortunately for some girls, periods aren't pain-free. Not everyone gets period pain, some people don't feel anything, others feel a slight heaviness in their lower tummy, and others get harsh cramps. Other side-effects can be sore boobs, back aches, head-aches, feeling dizzy and sick. As well as this, there's PMS (Pre-Menstrual Syndrome, also known as PMT or

Pre-Menstrual Tension) which affects some women. This can make you feel irritable, tearful, bloated, moody and depressed just before your period. If you're really unlucky, you can get the whole lot.

Tips

Pain To beat period pain, try over-the-counter remedies like Ponstan, which are specially designed for period pain.

Cramps If you have cramps, some people find it helps to curl up with a hot-water bottle.

Exercise Believe it or not, it does help to do some exercise, although you may not feel like it!

Caffeine Avoid caffeine in tea and coffee and cans of drink, to cut down on pain and bloating.

Water Drink plenty of water before your period to beat bloating.

Oil of Primrose Lots of people find taking Oil of Evening Primrose capsules helps period pain.

Get help If everything fails and you still get a lot of pain, don't be afraid to go to the doctor, as there are some treatments/medications for severe pain.

What to Use

There are loads of sanitary products on the market – just take a walk down the 'personal hygiene' aisle in the supermarket and you'll see everything from wings to wafer-thin pads. And yes it's a) embarrassing to buy them and b) your mum will have no idea of how embarrassing it is, and if you do ask her which ones are the best when shopping, she's likely to bellow down the shop, 'Do you want your panty pads this week, dear?' I think not. So here's a quick run-down on what to use:

Pads

Once upon a time, women had to use bits of rag when they had their period, and then wash them out for next month. Nice, eh? Nowadays though, pad technology has improved so much that they are tiny, thin and very, very discreet. Pads stick into your pants and lock in the blood as it comes out, so you don't feel it. They come in all shapes and sizes – with wings, contours, and millions of techno-babble names for their special soaking-up systems. Don't believe all the adverts, just try out a few brands to see which you get on better with. You pick different thicknesses for the differing flow of your period (generally they start light, get heavier, then ease off before stopping completely). There are special night-time pads, which are a bit thicker, as you wear them longer and no one sees anyway! Daytime pads should be changed every three or four hours.

Note Pads shouldn't really be thrown down the loo, you should wrap them in toilet paper and in public loos put them in the special bins by the side of the toilet. At home, you should wrap them up in the plastic wrapping they came in and put them in the bin.

Myth *They stink and everyone knows you're on.* Pads don't really smell enough for others to notice, but you should change them regularly, because if you left them for hours and hours they would start to whiff.

Pros There's no risk of Toxic Shock Syndrome and you don't have to learn how to insert them, like tampons.

Cons You can't go swimming and you do get a little bit of blood on the outside of your vagina.

Tampons

These are inserted into your vagina and soak up the blood internally. They come in various sizes from mini to super-plus, which is for the difference in blood flow, not the difference in vagina size! When you start your periods start with a mini, and then use a bigger size as your period becomes heavier. You can use ones with applicators, which are cardboard tubes, so you don't have to put your fingers inside, or you can use ones without – it's up to you. Paper applicators like Tampax are biodegradable, and can be flushed down the loo if there isn't a bin handy. There isn't much difference between brands, just find one you like.

Note You should always change your tampon at least every four to eight hours, as there is a rare condition called Toxic Shock Syndrome which can actually kill you if you leave a tampon in for days and days. Leaflets in tampon boxes explain it all, but if you feel sick, faint, get a temperature or body rash you should see a doctor immediately. If you are going to wear a tampon at night, put it in just before you go to sleep, and change it as soon as you wake up. If you are going to sleep for more than eight hours, it's best to use a pad.

Myth *Using a tampon takes your virginity.*
This is codswallop – it refers to breaking your hymen, which could happen if you forced a tampon

in, but as noted earlier in the chapter, most girls break their hymen naturally anyway. The hymen is a flexible membrane with a small opening through which the menstrual blood passes as it leaves your body – it's through this opening that your tampon can be inserted or removed. You don't lose your virginity until you've had sex.

Pros The plus-points to tampons is that no one knows you're having a period, you can still go swimming and they are more discreet than pads to carry about.

Cons You do have to learn to use them at the start – just follow the instructions in the boxes – and you should be aware of TSS.

What's Wrong?

Your periods are irregular and sometimes disappear

When you start your periods it can take up to a couple of years before they fall into a regular pattern. You can miss some and get two in one month. As long as there's no risk you could be pregnant, don't worry!

You miss a period

If you miss a period the first thing you must do is ask yourself if you could be pregnant. If you have had sex that month and you did not use contraception, or the condom could have split, you must see a doctor immediately.

If there is no way you could be pregnant, ask yourself some of the following questions:

- Have you been exercising a lot?
- Have you been on a very strict diet?
- Have you had a change in lifestyle – e.g. moving long distance?
- Are you very stressed about something, like exams, or have you suffered a trauma recently?

These are some of the reasons you can miss periods. Again, don't worry at first if there's no risk of pregnancy, but if you miss more than one, you should see a doctor.

Some athletes and girls who are severely underweight find their periods stop. This could cause problems long-term, so you must see your doctor if this happens to you.

Chapter 3

BOOBS

There's a funny thing about being a girl. You go through school, working out who you are, what you want and where you want to go in life, and then, one day, kerpow! You get boobs, and you suddenly notice that a) boys start talking to your bra instead of your face and b) you have a whole new set of worries about whether yours are big enough, too big, or non-existent. And blokes, well, are *obsessed* about them. It's quite sad really! Everywhere you look you see female celebs posing in their pants for sexy shoots, and 'Page Three Stunnas' whipping them out for all and sundry. Inside, you're shouting, 'Excuse me, but I have an interesting theory on crop rotations!' but all anyone else seems bothered about is how you fill out your jumper. OK, it isn't that bad, but it does take some getting used to when you first get boobs. So it is worth a chapter on this touchy subject, helping put any bosom worries to rest.

Size

The first, and biggest issue, is what size they'll be. You start getting boobs in puberty, but they don't finish growing until you're about eighteen or nineteen. And don't forget that if you put on or lose weight, they'll go with you. There's no way of guessing how big they will be – you can't even look to your mum for boob sizing, as you could have got those genes from either side of the family!

Big vs small

Believe me, despite hours of debate on the subject, there's no perfect breast size, and bigger is not better than smaller. It depends on you – your boobs are part of you, so try to be happy with whatever size they end up. Coming to terms with your body can take time, but if you start to have more confidence in yourself you might not feel it's so bad. Just as you fancy different boys, boys fancy girls of all shapes and sizes, no matter what the perfect media image might be!

There aren't any lotions or potions that can increase your breast size, and exercise may boost your pectoral muscles but won't enlarge your breasts. The best thing you can do is buy push-up or padded bras.

Boob problems

A few girls find that their boobs grow to be extremely large and become disproportionate to their body. This doesn't happen to many girls but occasionally breasts can get so big that they may cause severe back pain and discomfort and make it difficult to do day-to-day activities like running around. They can also make the girl very self-conscious and unhappy. If this happens, there is a breast reduction operation available on the NHS. If you can prove all of the above applies to you, and you have reached an age where your breasts have stopped growing, after many consultations with your doctor they may decide an operation is the right thing to do.

Lop-sided

As their boobs grow, lots of girls find that one gets bigger than the other. Sometimes one grows faster and then the other catches up. Virtually every girl has one boob that's slightly bigger than the other, but it's usually unnoticeable (the rest of your body isn't symmetrical either), but on rare occasions some girls are left with a distinct difference. If you are really worried, try wearing padded bras, and if that fails, you *can* speak to your doctor and possibly have surgery.

Nipples

You will find all through this book, that I keep saying every girl is different. And nipples are no exception. There's no perfect nipple – some girls have huge areolas (the area round the nipple) and tiny nipples, others have little areolas and huge nipples. Some are very dark brown, others are creamy-coloured. Some nipples are long and pointy, others short and stubby. Some point upwards, some droop downwards and others veer off to the sides. Some are inverted, which means they stick in rather than out. All nipples get hard when you're excited or cold.

Breast check

One very important thing you should remember is to get into the habit of checking your breasts throughout your life. Breast cancer isn't a big worry for teenagers, but it's good to make checks a habit. Check them by lying on your back with your right arm over your head, elbow bent. With the three middle fingers of your left hand, travel round your nipple feeling for unusual lumps, travelling in bigger and bigger circles. No part should feel hard. Repeat on the other side.

Bras

And finally, we reach the multi-million-pound business of changing your boob size and shape with the aid of the latest magical contraption. Bras can change the outline of your breasts substantially – you can wear push-up ones that make you look bigger, mini-misers that make you look smaller, and then hundreds of styles in between. Again, work out which ones suit you the best – there are different styles for different clothes – e.g. T-shirt bras with less seams, crop tops, demi-bras for low cut necklines and then zillions of back straps to choose from, like halter necks, cross-over backs, strapless . . . Just don't expect miracles, whatever the manufacturers say! It's very important to get the size right, for the correct support. You should get yourself measured by an expert – many department stores offer free measuring services. (And don't feel embarrassed – the bra-fitter will have seen every shape of breast under the sun!)

Chapter 4

BODY IMAGE

Now you have the info about your body and his body, before we can get anywhere near the nitty-gritty of sex, we should talk about body image. It's a sad fact of the modern world that a lot of people, mostly girls, have low self-esteem when it comes to body image. You see, we are bombarded by images of physical perfection on TV, billboards, magazines, catwalks and movies. These range from tall, skinny, androgynous models on the catwalks, to busty sex goddesses on the TV and in men's magazines. It's hard to know where you fit in yourself, and too many of us spend far too much time worrying that we don't measure up.

Remember this:

Weight There is no perfect weight. As long as you are healthy and keep yourself fit, you shouldn't worry about achieving a perfect weight.

Diets It is medically proven that crash diets do not work. The only way to lose weight is to eat a healthy, balanced diet and take plenty of exercise. Miracle products like slimming pills or meal replacement drinks don't really work long-term, not that it stops people trying – the diet product industry is worth billions of pounds a year in the UK. What a waste!

THE IMAGE TESTER

Circle the number in the Yes or No column in answer to the following questions and add up your final score to see which type you are:

	Yes	No
1 Do you like your body generally?	3	0
2 Would you consider plastic surgery if it was free?	0	1
3 Would you like a make-over?	1	2

	Yes	**No**
4 Do you wish you had more confidence?	1	3
5 Do your mates pay you compliments?	1	0
6 In shops, can you find lots of styles that suit you?	3	1
7 Do you want different colour hair?	1	2
8 Are you jealous of your mates' looks?	0	2
9 Are you regularly on a diet?	1	2
10 Do you think your life would change if you looked different?	0	3
11 Do you spend a lot of money on beauty and hair products?	1	2
12 Do you ever avoid looking in mirrors?	0	1
13 Do you think boys might fancy you?	2	0
14 Is there something you'd like to change about your looks?	1	2
15 Are you on a diet now?	1	3
16 Do you usually wear black rather than bright colours?	0	2
17 Are you comfortable in a swimming costume?	3	0
18 Would you say you followed fashion closely?	2	1
19 Are you confident with boys?	3	0
20 Do people say you're fun?	3	0

	Yes	No
21 Do you get a lot of male attention?	3	0
22 Do you always wear make-up before you go out?	1	2
23 Do you go shopping every Saturday?	1	2
24 Would you say you're fat?	0	2
25 Do you hide one part of your body?	1	2

1-14 points - Bitter

You have very low self-esteem and body image. You don't like much about yourself at all, and you think the main problem is your body. Whether it's that you think you're fat, have a big nose, big legs, too skinny, horrible hair or sticky-out ears, you're so self-conscious about it that you scuttle away any time someone tries to talk to you. The thing is, real happiness comes from within, and the more you like yourself for being you, the more attractive you become to everyone else. Honestly. Think about all those pop stars and actors that are, quite frankly, ugly, but because they carry themselves with so much confidence they ooze charisma and so seem attractive. That's how it works! So forget planning that liposuction, nose job, or miracle diet, and start liking yourself and you'll see an instant change.

15-27 points - Bashful

The good news is that you don't have a big problem about yourself. You quite like who you are and you have lots of plans about where you want to go in your life. The bad news is that you are so shy you daren't let anyone see the real you. You have loads to offer the world – you have a lot of good friends, and you are well-liked, even though you won't believe that yourself. You just need to have more confidence in yourself. The happier and more confident you appear, the more attractive you are to everyone else. And that's the key – some people spend thousands of pounds on plastic surgery, fancy diets or designer clothes, but if you are not confident within yourself, you won't shine out. So believe in it, baby!

28-39 points - Bothered

This is probably the most ticked category. You are quite a happy-go-lucky person in general. You make an effort to look good, and you dabble in a few diets when you think you need a bit of a trim-down. There's quite a few bits about yourself you don't like and you do worry about them a bit too much. You love clothes and you know all the tricks of the trade to minimise the bits that bother you – like black to slim down pear-shaped hips, or low waists to hide a pot belly. There's nothing out of the ordinary here, but just keep a check on yourself; if you find yourself becoming unhappy about the way you look and starting to get obsessed by one particular thing, take time to chill out and reflect on everything in your life, not just your image.

40+ points – Balanced

Congratulations! You are a super-balanced person. You are happy with who you are, starting from within and ending with the way you look. Other people are drawn to you like a magnet, because you exude confidence, sexuality and happiness. You do get bad days, of course, but you usually draw on your inner strength to get you through. The thing is, you may not actually have a supermodel-perfect body, but you don't give a damn, because you like who you are, don't you? Everyone else can learn so much from you. You have great personal style, and you're not bothered about what is the latest thing to wear – you wear what you like, and always carry it off. Way to go, girl!

Chapter 5

BODY Q&A

Have I started?
I recently found a brown discharge in my pants. I haven't started my periods yet, but this didn't look like blood. What is it?

This *is* your period. When you start your periods for the first time they often look like thick brown goo, not like blood. This is just the start – it's simply your body getting used to its new function. After a few months it will look like ordinary blood and the flow will increase. You should start using sanitary pads or a tampon now. You'll find that your periods will take quite a long time to regulate themselves into a cycle, but it's quite normal.

What's in my pants?
I have a white discharge in my knickers. It's really embarrassing, what should I do?

This is normal. Everyone has vaginal discharge, which is just the vagina cleaning itself by producing this mix of mucus, cells and bacteria. Normal discharge is wet, clear to white in colour, is not itchy and doesn't smell. It may turn yellowish as it dries in your pants. It's one of those things no one talks about, but every woman gets discharge – the amount varies according to your menstrual cycle. However, if you notice that your discharge changes colour and/or gets lumpier and starts to smell, you must go to see a doctor, because these are symptoms of infections.

What is a smear?
Someone told me you should have a smear to see if you have cancer. But what is one?

A pap smear is a test a doctor or nurse does to see if you have cervical cancer. They insert a specu-lum into your vagina to hold the walls of the vagina apart, have a look inside to make sure everything is healthy, and then insert a swab to take a few cells from your cervix. This is sent to a lab, to see if there are any abnormal cells that require treatment.

Sounds painful It isn't painful, but the more tense you are the higher the risk of slight discomfort.

Do both male and female doctors do smears? Yes. However if you feel uncomfortable with a male doctor, you can ask for a female doctor, or nurses at your local surgery can do this, or you could go to a family planning clinic.

When do I need one? You need to start having smears three years after you first have sex, then every three to five years after that.

Nipple worry

One of my nipples sticks in and the other sticks out. It comes out sometimes, but always goes back in again. I'm really worried there's something wrong with me.

There's nothing abnormal about this. All nipples and boobs are different, even from each other on the same girl, just as you discovered. You have what's called an inverted nipple. It may come back out permanently as you get older, or it may not, but it won't make any difference to your life – either in sex, or breast-feeding a baby eventually.

Smelly bits

I think I smell down below. I'm really ashamed. What can I do – can I use any perfumes or deodorants?

First off, every girl has a natural odour from her vagina. As long as you wash regularly, there shouldn't be a problem. Check that you don't have any coloured or thick discharge, which could result from an infection like thrush (candida), and could account for the smell. Otherwise, don't worry about it. Never, ever use deodorant, perfumes, or strongly perfumed soaps around your vagina as it's very sensitive and you would cause severe irritation.

I'm late

I have missed a period. I don't think I could be pregnant, as I used a condom when I had sex, so what could it be?

There are several reasons why you could be late. The first and most urgent one to check off, is pregnancy. If you have had sex since your last period, do a pregnancy test or go to the doctor for one immediately. Even if you used a condom there could have been an accident, it could have broken or torn without you realising. If you haven't had sex, then it could be down to hormones, stress, dieting or over-exercising. If your period doesn't come next month it would be wise to see a doctor anyway.

Itchy and scratchy

My vagina is itchy and I am scared that I've got nits or something. Please help – it's really embarrassing.

This itchiness is most likely to be thrush, which is a yeast infection of your vagina, and can be easily treated with a cream or pessary like Canesten. You can buy these products at the chemist, but if you are unsure, you should see your doctor. It's not very likely that you have got nits in your pubic hair, as you would be able to see them. If it is neither of the above, please see your doctor who'll be able to help.

Tampon tester

I have recently started my periods, and am using tampons. But I don't think I am using them right, as half of it shows once I have put it in. Please help.

It sounds as though you're not inserting the tampon far enough. Look inside the box the tampons come in and read the leaflet. It shows you how to insert it properly. You should not be able to feel it once it is inside you, and only the thread should be showing. Just try to relax and you should have more success.

Pube-ing question

How much hair are you meant to have? I'm really worried because my pubic hair is so bushy I think I'm abnormal. When I go swimming it pokes out the side of my costume; I'm too ashamed to go any more.

The answer is that there's no normal amount of pubes to have – some people have huge thatches of hair, and some have just a few wisps – just as some pubic hair is thick and wiry, and some wispy and thin. Firstly, don't feel like you're abnormal, as many women have bits of hair peeping out the sides of their costumes. Secondly, if you're worried about your pubic hair showing, just remove its outer edges at the tops of your legs, by shaving or waxing.

Love bites

What actually is a love bite, and is it dangerous?

A love bite is when someone sucks on your skin firmly with their mouth, and leaves a red bruise there. It's not dangerous, but it doesn't look that nice, especially when it's somewhere really noticeable, like your neck! People tend to do them as a bit of a 'look at me, I've been saucy' statement, but then end up wearing a scarf until they fade . . .

Chapter 6

ATTRACTION

So, you've read through the whole of the Body & You section, and feel fully confident about all the functions of your bits and bobs. Now we're on to the emotional part of sex and attraction. This is where it all gets complicated. You see, the rules of emotions and attraction are this: there are no rules. The whole boy and girl thing can be very confusing – from how to tell if he fancies you, how to work out if you fancy him, and then what on earth to do if both of you fancy each other and you start getting all sorts of frisky feelings!

That's what this chapter is about – helping you work out what you are feeling, and hopefully, what he is too.

WHAT IS ATTRACTION?

Attraction is when you are drawn towards someone else. Sometimes this can be plainly physical – you think someone is absolutely gorgeous and you feel all manner of sexual attraction towards them, and you feel like it is overpowering your brain. Or, it could be mental stimulation, you may think that person is really interesting and you know you want to talk to them more and more. Or it could be both. It boils down to knowing you want to see someone again, because you can't get them out of your mind, and they make you feel sort of special when you are around them.

How do you know if you fancy someone?

The answer is, you don't – you just know you feel funny when they're around, and you know you want to feel funny for longer! You may feel nervous, ecstatically happy, flustered – but generally you will be feeling lots of things, much more strongly than usual.

Reality isn't like a movie where the moment your eyes meet an orchestra pops up with a well-timed ballad. However there are a few classic symptoms of fancying someone – your heart beats fast or jumps a second, you may feel light-headed, short of breath, you get butterflies in your tummy, and you start sweating. Everywhere. You might find you can't help looking at him and you seem unable to string a sentence togther.

Your attractor factor

Ask yourself the following questions:

- Am I alive?
- Am I human?

Hopefully, the answer to these taxing teasers is yes. Yes, it's nonsense – but the point is that too many of us get hung-up about whether we are attractive to the opposite sex. We spend millions of pounds on fancy outfits and beauty products, read countless magazine articles on how to pull, when the secret is – be happy. Honestly, that's all it takes. Be happy in yourself, and you'll draw people to you like a magnet. Like who you are, where you're going and what you look like, and bingo, everyone else does too. Think about it – your mates always say, 'It's always the same – whenever I get a boyfriend, I get asked out by other boys.' And you know why? Because when they have a boyfriend, they're happy, confident, feel liked and appreciated. They are really relaxed, which radiates out to anyone else they meet, who then thinks, 'Hmm, this girl's fun to be around. She knows who she is, and isn't trying too hard. I think I'll have a bit of that.' Simple as that! The trick is to make yourself remember to feel happy when you're not, which isn't simple, but just try to think of the following things:

• Remember back to the last time you were really happy – how did you feel?

• What things make you feel really positive? (Plans for the future, thinking of nice things that have happened, etc . . .)

Then hopefully, even when you are feeling low in self-confidence, you can draw on better times and pull yourself up to a happier level, which in the end, makes you more appealing to others.

How do you know if boys fancy you?

At *Bliss*, this is the most frequently asked question on our problem pages. It's really hard to read some boys' minds and work out if they do fancy you and are just being shy, or if they don't have any feelings towards you. They often send out a bewildering array of messages – from avoiding eye contact and acting supercool, to popping up every time you go somewhere and then blushing lots, showing off and being childish, or even teasing you quite harshly. The answer we give is always the same – the only way to find out if he fancies you is to talk to him. This doesn't mean rushing up, shrieking, 'Will you snog me?' before you've even been introduced, but just means that if you strike up a conversation about anything, you are opening up the possibilities of a relationship. You are giving yourself a chance to see if you have many things in common, and if a spark is lit between you.

Use your intuition – do you feel attracted to him after talking to him, and does he appear to enjoy talking to you? If you think he does, and he just isn't asking you out, then he may be shy, and it's worth you asking him. Boys don't get given manuals on pulling girls at birth, you know, so they are as much in the dark as we are. The worse thing that could happen is he says no, in which case you just shrug it off and get on with your life. Go for it! On the other hand, if you really don't feel anything between you, then it's best to keep the relationship as friends for a while longer, and give yourself time to work out if there's anything there.

Chapter 7

SEXUALITY

So, we've worked out what goes where in the Body & You section, and now we have to work out what's going on inside of you. Welcome to the wonderful world of sexuality. Once you start getting sexual feelings it's often difficult to talk about them to anyone. So here are some of the most-asked questions about sexual feelings:

I keep dreaming about sex – with really weird people like my teacher, or my mate's dad. I'm so ashamed – I don't think like this in the daytime. What's wrong with me?

Firstly, nothing is wrong with you. You're a normal teenager, having normal dreams. Your hormones get up to all sorts of things through your teenage years, and rude dreams are just one way they pop up. You often have dreams about having sex with people that figure in your everyday life, but it doesn't mean that you really fancy them. It doesn't mean you're dirty, or sex-mad, or anything, honestly! The only trouble is you have to face them the next day and you panic that they know what you've been dreaming. But believe me, they don't. I hope . . .

I have a huge crush on this pop singer. I know I'm being stupid, but I can't help myself and I'm becoming so obsessed with him I can't concentrate on school or anything. How can I stop myself?

Well, I think you are part of the way there, because you have already acknowledged that this is a crush, rather than love, or any kind of viable relationship. The thing about crushes is that they can be great – your imagination paints lovely scenarios for you to go daydreaming off into, but that's all it is – imagination. The bad part is, as you say, when you can't stop thinking about this person and imagining that you really will get together. You just have to think rationally and write down a list of all the reasons why this would never work. Once you acknowledge it, boys in the real world look a far better option!

I can't stop thinking about sex. Help!

Firstly, stop worrying, thinking about sex is normal, and part of every teenager's life. Your hormones are in overdrive right now, and one way you can spot they're raging is by your thoughts turning to sex, say, every ten seconds. It's just the result of your body trying to get used to all these new emotions and feelings that are coursing through it. It doesn't mean you are sex-mad, gagging for a bit of action wherever you can get it, it just means you are *normal*. The best thing you can do is stop worrying and make sure you fill your day with plenty of activities and interests that can prise your mind away from the dirty deed!

I have had cyber-sex with someone in a chat room. I'm really ashamed. I've never even had a boyfriend in real life. Am I a pervert?

No, you are not a pervert. The Internet has brought with it a whole new way of meeting people, secretly. You can be who you want to be in cyberspace, and no one knows. What you have done is what hundreds of people do every day – let your inhibitions down, and discovered what turns you on. There's nothing to be ashamed about in this, but what you should think about carefully is that while cyber-sex is safe sex in that you can't catch anything and it's at a 'safe' distance from your 'real' life, you could pick up a pervert as there's no way of knowing who you were really talking to. Never give anyone your address, name, or any way of identifying you, and if the conversations get too heavy or weird, log off immediately.

I looked at my brother's porn mags and found myself getting turned on. Am I weird, or even lesbian?

So many of us think that any kind of arousal must mean we are weird. Of course you aren't – you are just getting to know what turns you on. Looking at sexy images of women in porn magazines doesn't mean you are literally a lesbian, because it can be more about imagining yourself in those positions, or yourself being sexually desirable to boys, than actually fancying the women in the pictures. Porn itself provokes a lot of different responses from different people (see Chapter 8), but if looking at these images helps you understand your own sexual desires and responses, then it is a positive thing. Of course, if you know that you like looking at pictures of women because you fancy them, then that can help you come to terms with your own sexuality. There is more on this subject on pages 53–55.

My boyfriend asked me to tell him my fantasies, but I can't, because I don't have any. What are they?

Fantasies are when you imagine a situation, or act out a little scene in your head to turn yourself on. Not everyone does this – and if you don't have any sexual thoughts or fantasies, then that's perfectly normal too. Everyone has their own level of sexual interest and activity and you should never feel pressurised into either doing anything you don't want to, or being anything that you are not.

But I have loads of fantasies, and some of them are really dirty. So does that make me a perve?

No, it doesn't make you a pervert. Again, everyone has their own levels of interest in sex, and fantasies are a good way of working out what turns you on, and how to respond to your own desires. The thing about fantasies is that they are often completely separate from reality. People have all sorts of fantasies from the straightforward to the bizarre, but it doesn't mean they really want to act them all out. That's something you'll work out in your own time, depending on what you feel comfortable with in 'real life'.

Masturbation

OK, so we've admitted that we get turned on, and we understand why that is. So now, what do we do when we start getting aroused? Nothing – maybe. Run around and do lots of other things to distract your mind – possibly, or . . . masturbate. You'll probably read this and laugh. OK, masturbation is not a topic to bring up at the dinner table. Hardly anyone admits to doing it, but believe me, loads of people do. Boys are well up front about their wanking habits – but girls, no, we girls would like everyone to believe that we are permanently residing in a Jane Austen novel, and never a dirty thought should sully our mind. Which is a load of rubbish, quite obviously.

What

Masturbation, or self-stimulation, is when you bring yourself to orgasm or get yourself turned on, on your own.

How

Girls do it in many ways. They rub their fingers around their clitoris, use their fingers inside their vagina, use a jet of water from the tap or shower

51

against their clitoris, rub themselves against a pillow, squeeze their legs together in a rhythm, look at magazines, read books, fantasise, or use dildos/vibrators or other objects inside them.

Why

It brings release if you are feeling turned on or frustrated. Masturbation is the ultimate safe sex. You can't get pregnant or catch a disease. It also helps you figure out what feels good for you, and helps you understand your body and the way you respond when you are turned on. You can give yourself an orgasm, and see what it feels like. Then when you do eventually have sex with someone, you understand yourself, and you can tell them what you like and don't like.

Why not

But masturbation doesn't have to be for everyone. If you don't want to do it, then fine – it doesn't mean that you are frigid (won't enjoy sex), or make you a worse lover in the future. Other factors everyone should remember are: don't do it anywhere you can be caught – it's highly embarrassing; don't use any objects inside you that are sharp, or could break, and make sure your fingers are clean and don't rub too violently or you could slightly irritate your skin.

Myths

There are millions of myths associated with masturbation – it makes you go blind, it'll make you infertile and you'll get hairy palms, for example. Obviously they aren't true. There are no dangers with masturbation, and it doesn't have any side-effects. You could say it's healthy for you, because it stops you having sex with the wrong people just to enjoy or release sexual feelings. One other myth is that you only do it when you don't have a boyfriend. This isn't the case – if you want to do it, then carry on. Many couples use masturbation as part of their love-making as well – to each other, or to themselves in front of each other.

Gay vs Straight

As you develop your sexual self, you start to work out what and who turns you on. A lot of girls start to look at other girls in a sexual way in their teens, and this can range from having crushes on other girls, or women you know, to being fascinated by a female celebrity. These feelings could be the result of the intensity of your admiration for a role model, wanting to be like them, or they could be sexual feelings – time will reveal this to you as your feelings for this and other women change and develop. As you take time to work out who you are, you may decide that you are gay or bisexual. If you know you are, without a doubt, gay, then that's one important decision already made for you. If you feel confused, the one thing you should always remember is that through your teens you have a lot of conflicting emotions and feelings, and one of these is often sexuality. You can have 'crushes' on girls, and fantasise about them, without it meaning you are definitely gay. Take time to work out what your true feelings are – only you know how you really feel inside. Remember:

• Your sexuality does not have to be defined once only – it can and does change over time.

• Don't bother pressurising yourself into labelling yourself. You are you – you don't have to define yourself as gay, straight or bisexual.

• Don't feel pressured into having sexual relations with anyone – male or female – to prove anything to yourself or anyone else.

• If you feel confused, confide in people you trust.

• If you need to talk through your feelings, or if you

want any help or advice, call the Lesbian & Gay Switchboard on 020 7837 7324.

Homophobia

Unfortunately our society is not as completely open about people's sexuality as it should be, and if you do decide you're gay, and want to come out, then you should be prepared for some adverse reactions from people. Try not to put too much pressure on yourself to label yourself and to tell others until you feel very, very sure you're ready for the world!

Chapter 8

ATTITUDES TO SEX

As you read through this book you should, hopefully, be gaining an insight into the way you feel about yourself, your body and sex. That's the easy part. Now, you have to work out what you really believe in, and hold true to it, despite all the pressures and mixed messages you get bombarded with every day from the outside world. We still live in a very hypocritical society. As a teenage girl, you're told that good girls just don't have sex, but then you switch on the TV and everyone seems to be at it. Sex is used to sell everything, from mobile phones to men's magazines, movies to tabloids. It can be really confusing. The decisions you make about sex should always be yours. However, when things like religion, cultural beliefs and the law come into it, it makes it harder to find your own path through sexuality. You only have yourself to answer to in the end, so no matter how much pressure you get from any quarters, try to be true to you.

Family Pressure

Your family background and upbringing forms the base of all your thoughts about sex and intimacy. It leaves more of an impression than you think. For example, your parents may have a very loving relationship, and show affection in front of you all the time. Then it's likely you will be comfortable and affectionate to your boyfriend or partner. If your parents are very reserved and don't show any affection in front of you, it's likely you'd be uncomfortable with open displays of affection in your own love life.

When it comes to sex, everyone's parents are different, and no one is perfect, believe me. You may have super-open parents who discuss sex and contraception with you at an early age. You may like this or you may think your parents are beatnik loonies. On the other hand, you may have parents who would rather scale Mount Everest in their swimsuits than approach the topic of sex and you having it. If you can have a sensible conversation about sex with your parents this is, of course, the best option, but if not, turn to older sisters or brothers, friends or even friends' liberal parents when you need someone to talk to for information, reassurance or advice.

How to bring up the subject of sex

Pick your time Don't blurt out, 'I'm having it off!' when Mum's stuffing a turkey. Find a time when everyone's relaxed and alert (so not at mid-night, when Dad's passed out in front of the TV).

Target Pick the parent who is most likely to be cool about it, and tackle them alone. Don't try to talk to them both, or it'll be like a school presentation on a report they're not ready to hear.

They'll blab Oh yes, and be prepared – because whichever one you tell will *always* tell the other one, even if they are divorced and hate the sight of each other, and no matter what promises they swore to you.

Keep calm and present your case sensibly. For example, 'Mum, I'm sixteen now, and I'm sure you know that I'm bound to have sex sooner or later. I just wanted to talk about contraception . . .' Not, 'I'm not a child, you know!' before running off

sobbing because they banned Baz from sleeping
in your bed.

Respect them If they really can't deal with it,
and won't let your boyfriend within a thirty-kilometre
radius of the house, show them you respect their
wishes, and eventually they may change their minds.

Peer Pressure

One of the biggest reasons why people start having
sex is because their mates do. Teenage years are full
of experimentation, and so many people end up in
sexual situations because they've heard their mates
bragging about something, and thought they had to
do it to get cred. The only reason you should ever
do anything sexual with anyone, is because you one
hundred per cent want to, feel ready, and know you
are trusted and respected by the other person.

The sex scoreboard

Have you ever been in the situation where some
bright spark comes up and says, 'Have you got to
Number Six yet?' If your peers run a sex scoreboard,
then you'll know exactly what I mean. You stand
there floundering, thinking, 'Do I say yes or no?',
and even when you take a gamble and say no, you still

have to discreetly discover that Number Six equals a blowjob or something. This is a classic case of friends making it the norm to tick off how far you've been with a boy, like it's a competition. If you find yourself doing anything just to score higher than your mates, then you're not doing it for the right reasons.

Answer back If your mates always hassle you, saying, 'How far have you gone?' just answer back something like, 'Clacton's my limit with my bus pass, thanks,' and keep well out of it.

Boys Remember that despite what he says, most teenage boys are trying to notch up points on their own scoreboards, so never let him go further than *you* want.

Regrets If you do get carried away, and go further than you wanted just to say you'd done it, then don't beat yourself up about it. Even if people gossip, act above them all, and remember that you never have to do anything again, just because you did it once.

Keep out of it The best way to put your mates/peers off if they start saying who's been further and pressuring you to join in, is to keep your distance. Act mysterious, divert them with jokes, answer in a flippant manner, or just plain lie. But the best way to get them to shut up is to turn the questions back to them – every single time.

Media Messages

As I said, sex plays a huge part in the media. It sells everything from beer cans to cars, make-up and perfume to music and movies. It also sells TV programmes, books, newspapers and magazines. With so many images of sex around, these can define how some people think of sex – for example, a lot of men and women think Page Three models have the ultimate female bodies, whereas others think supermodels are the epitome of physical perfection. This can be annoying as obviously, women don't just come in two varieties – big boob sex-bombs or cat-walk queens – so it's up to us to work out our own definitions of sexy.

Although it's easy to say, try not to get too hung-up on what is beautiful, or what is sexy. Remember that the images you see of models and actresses are not real life. For a start, they have a whole team of stylists working on getting the look perfect, plus special lighting and camera angles. As well as that, in magazines most of the cover models have had their imperfections digitally removed on a computer. Real sexiness comes from confidence within.

Porn

Having said that sex sells everything, there's also media that sells sex – porn. Everything from shops to videos, magazines, movies and websites exist to peddle sexual images and fantasies to people. Whether you agree with it or not is up to you, but it's a multi-million-pound industry based on women and men showing their bits in order to excite the reader/viewer. Some people say that it exploits and degrades women and some say that it shows women have control over men, because they are making so much money out of showing parts of their bodies which, after all, everyone has. The thing to remember is it is all sexual fantasy, and it is not about real life or real relationships, in which women have much more to offer than simply their bodies.

Sex And The Law

Sex under sixteen is illegal

In England, Scotland and Wales, sex under the age of sixteen is illegal. In Northern Ireland, the legal age of consent is seventeen. If you are under sixteen, and thinking about sex, remember that it is illegal. OK, so there aren't sex police who pop up at the end of your bed and nick you if you get frisky, but the law is there to protect you. Under sixteen, most of us are still working out what's going on with our lives, emotions and bodies, and having sex too soon can have long-lasting damaging effects to your mind, and your body, as you may not be physically or emotionally ready.

According to the law, if girls have sex under sixteen, they can't be prosecuted, but the boy or man can, even if she agreed. Interestingly, if a girl or woman had sex with a boy who was under sixteen (but she was older), then under the Sexual Offences Act 1956 she could be prosecuted only for indecent assault.

Gay Sex

In Britain, the legal age to have gay sex, for two men, is eighteen. Campaigners are trying to get it brought down to sixteen, the same as heterosexual sex. Under the Sexual Offences Act 1967 sexual contact between men is permitted only if both men consent, are eighteen or over, and it takes place in private with no one else present. Believe it or not, if you are lesbian, there is no minimum age for having sex. The story goes that this is because when the laws were brought in, in Queen Victoria's reign, she refused to believe that lesbians existed, so made no law against them.

Anal sex

In another loophole, anal sex between a man and a woman in England and Wales is illegal under the age of eighteen. In Scotland it's illegal under sixteen, and in Northern Ireland it's plain illegal!

Prostitution

Although it is known as the world's oldest profession, sex for money is illegal. Some people debate that it's a business agreement between two adults, whereas others say it is degrading to women and morally wrong.

Chapter 9

ARE YOU A SEXPERT?

Are you a sexual expert or a love learner? Take our true/false tester to discover just how clued-up you really are.

Read the following statements and tick whether you think they are true or false. At the end, check against the right answers and add up your score of correct answers to discover your sex knowledge.

1. Condoms are available free from family planning clinics.   T ☑ F ☐

2. The areola is the area round a woman's nipple.   T ☐ F ☐

3. If you douche with cola after sex you won't get pregnant.   T ☐ F ☐

4. You can catch HIV from kissing.   T ☐ F ☐

5. You can get pregnant in the middle of your period. T ☐ F ☐

6. You can't get pregnant the first time you have sex. T ☐ F ☐

7. There is a condom for women. T ☐ F ☐

8. You're not a virgin if your hymen is broken. T ☐ F ☐

9. Oral sex is the term for talking dirty. T ☐ F ☐

10. If a guy gets a hard-on and doesn't have sex/wank, it could be dangerous. T ☐ F ☐

11. The Fallopian tube is what you wee through. T ☐ F ☐

12. Masturbating can make you blind or infertile. T ☐ F ☐

13. The clitoris is located inside the vagina. T ☐ F ☐

14. The missionary position is where a boy has sex lying on top of a girl. T ☐ F ☐

15. You could get pregnant if you swallow sperm. T ☐ F ☐

How did you score?

1 T	2 T	3 F	4 F	5 T	6 F	7 T	8 F
9 F	10 F	11 F	12 F	13 F	14 T	15 F	

Check your correct score by the categories below:

5 and under – Love L-plates

You need a crash course in love lingo before you can think of going further with a boy. You know the basics, i.e. what goes where and what happens, but that's about it. Gen up on as much info as you can get your hands on, and you'll feel more confident when people start talking about sex and won't feel too embarrassed to own up and say you don't know what something is. So many people end up getting themselves into silly situations because they don't want to look stupid in front of their mates. Remember, knowledge really is power!

6-10 – Love lieutenant

You're about average. You're well clued-up on most of the facts of life, and you'll often be found explaining facts to your mates. You know all the basics, and you know a lot of helpful information as well, such as where you get contraception, and what you should use. A lot of your mates look up to you, because you seem to have all the answers – but what they don't know is sometimes you get a bit confused – avoid the temptation to ad lib if you don't know the answer! There are a few gaping holes in your love dictionary that would be better filled, as you can never know too much – a lot of the world's most sensible girls still make mistakes.

10 and over – Love master

Well done – you are really clued-up when it comes to the facts of life. You are not one to get sidetracked by myths and gossip, but know the plain facts and like to tell them to your mates. You may not have actually experienced much, or anything yourself, but you have made it your business to find out all the info first, so that if and when you decide to have a physical relationship, it will be on your terms. But a word of warning – you can never know too much, and the facts can still be swept away in the heat of the moment. So be true to yourself – if you've made the effort to learn all this, use it wisely.

Chapter 10

BOYS AND SEX

Now, it's all very well us girls getting so clued-up that we're walking sexual health directories, but has anyone told the boys what it's all about? Boys are traditionally a few years behind girls in puberty, and some might argue they remain that way for the rest of their lives! Bless. But we should never forget that boys have to get their sex info from somewhere, and where do you think they find the best place for that is? – yes, their mates. So it doesn't take a brainiac to work out that if all their sex info is coming from their mates, maybe it's not the most reliable source in the world. Because boys don't sit around for endless 'Dawson's Creek'-style emotional discussions, do they? No, their sex conversations are going to be less of the 'which mode of contraception is most reliable' type and more of the 'did you give her one?' variety. Which means that they know even less about the mysteries of love, sex and relationships than we do. Damn!

DOUBLE STANDARDS

For years and years girls and boys have existed with double standards when it comes to sex. You know – if a girl has sex with a lot of boys, then she's a slapper, but if a boy has sex with a lot of girls he's a stud. When you think about it, it's ridiculous – if it's actually good for a boy to be getting a lot of action, he has to find someone to get the action with, so how come those girls are looked down on? There's no easy explanation for this outdated attitude. Maybe it harks back to days of maidens and knights and chastity belts! Or maybe society likes to label people and gets a bit scared of women who are in control of their own sexual destiny. The important thing for you to remember is not to listen to nonsense gossip like this, and not to fuel it yourself. Whatever you choose to do yourself, do it with dignity. Never do anything to look good, but only because you believe it is the right course of action to take, and you are one hundred per cent sure that you will cope with whatever happens, or is said, afterwards.

Boys' scoreboards

When boys are discovering sex, they are experiencing slightly different emotions to us. They begin, as we've already discussed, by getting erections willy-nilly and wet dreams, and discovering this wonderful new toy which hangs between their legs. And their main ambition is to give this new toy a good rogering.

OK, this is a gross generalisation, but through puberty boys' hormones are running wild, and their main sex hormone, testosterone, is quite rampant at this time, hence boys' constant thoughts about sex. And so some boys, while they do, of course, have very strong feelings for you, would give anything to get their leg over. They are discovering love, and lust, and emotions, the same as you, but they are also being egged on by their mates, discussing how far each of them has gone, and who's done what with which girl. You know the sex scoreboard we discussed in Chapter 8 – well of course boys are operating on this scoreboard too. They may not tell you that, but there's a big chance they'll tell their mates how far they went, and even invent results if it comes to it.

Boys are under a lot of pressure themselves, with their mates egging them on while they try to make sense of their own emotions and feelings. The worst thing for a boy is to admit he got knocked back, which is where you find rumours starting that so-and-so shagged so-and-so, when they may not have even said hello. This also explains why sometimes boys are sweet and kind to you in private and then act all macho and horrible in front of their mates. You may disagree with the whole of this paragraph, and know boys who are not like this at all, but it's worth being prepared.

Name-calling

The bad side of sexual relationships, or sometimes any relationships with boys can be the name-calling. Some boys are sadly too immature to be having sex, and it is these boys (see above) who end up as right pains. Say no, or say yes to these boys and you could find yourself being called:

Frigid This is a term for someone who has no sexual feelings and can't have a healthy sex life. You'll usually hear it used as an insult to someone who has just turned down the name-caller.

It actually reflects more on the name-caller than the person they're hassling.

Slag This is the opposite of frigid, and is meant to refer to a girl who has had sex with a lot of people. You'll hear it bandied about by a boy who perhaps had his way (or maybe didn't?) with you and then dropped you (or you dropped him). If people say this to you, hold your head up high and keep quiet about everything. They'll soon move on to the next scandal.

Bike This is another term for slag, but usually refers to someone who's had sex with a few boys who know each other. You'll hear it applied to girls, as in, 'Oh her – she's just the town bike.' This is really sad and cruel, so the best thing to do if it's applied to you is, again, rise above it, remove yourself from anywhere where they can keep calling you names, and try to show that it doesn't affect you at all.

Nympho This is the shortened term for nymphomaniac, which means someone addicted to sex. You'll find it's a slightly nicer way of saying someone's a slag. Hardly anyone really is addicted to sex, and it's more likely this term is used about a woman who enjoys sex and isn't ashamed of that fact. If you hear it, think of some cutting remark to

73

say back, like, 'Nympho? Darling, if you were the last man on earth I'd take a vow of chastity . . .'

What's inside boys' heads

The good news is that boys are as self-conscious and afraid as you are. While they may hide it with a bit of male bravado, most boys worry about all the same things girls do – do they smell? are their bodies good enough? and in a sex situation, is their tackle normal and will their partner notice they're not very experienced and they're nervous? So that's comforting.

A big worry for boys is that their willy isn't big enough. There's so much nonsense spouted about penis size (by boys to each other) that most of them are really hung-up about whether theirs comes up to scratch or not. Add to that the anxiety about whether they can please you in bed, can they go on long enough, what positions are they meant to be in, etc. and you have one very worried young man. The best way to alleviate yours and his fears is through communication. Talk about what you both want from the relationship, about what you both think about sex and what turns you both on. That way you enter into a sexual relationship with honesty, and you should both leave it with what you want.

Chapter 11

THINGS BOYS SAY TO GET YOU INTO BED

We girls hear a lot of rubbish in our time – and none more than when some little eager blokey is trying to get into our pants. Now, in most cases boys are fairly sensible and straightforward about their desires and you can both make up your minds together about whether you want to take it one step further and roll around in the nearest haystack. But some of the little souls decide that the best way to get you to drop all your clothes is to spin you a few yarns. So for your eyes only, here are the top ten tall tales told by boys to get you into bed:

1. My balls will turn blue

This is a classic. It's usually said when he's extremely turned on and has a raging erection, and he's trying to persuade you to administer to it, or him. Boys reckon they can convince girls that there will be a medical problem if you leave their willy hard – i.e. their balls will turn blue because of the lack of use, supposedly. It doesn't take a genius to work out that this is codswallop – nothing happens if you leave an erection, except that the penis just goes back to normal. And the only time his little balls will turn blue is if they are excessively cold.

2. My willy will drop off

This is a variation on the one above – his argument here is that if you leave his willy in a state of erection, it will break or, at worst, drop off because of this highly dangerous state. Again this is rubbish – nothing will happen if you leave it, don't worry!

3. It's bad for me if you don't

If numbers one and two were a bit obvious, our plucky guy may use this line, in a vague medical reference to what would happen if you didn't sort him out when he's so turned on. This comes from the incredible tension and frustration he's feeling when he has an erection or is feeling horny. The blood is pumping round his genitals and he's literally gagging for some action. That's all that's 'wrong' with him. True, if you did give him an orgasm it would relieve him immensely, but likewise if you left him alone for a few minutes he would calm down quite easily and no harm would come of anything.

4. We'll just lay down together

Moving off from the medical complaints, this classic quote is often used by boys trying to persuade you to go to bed with them. What they are suggesting is, let's go and lay down on the bed together and then just go to sleep. What they mean is, let's go and lay down on the bed together, then start kissing and caressing, and then eventually when I've got you in the mood I'll try my luck again.

The occasional boy might actually mean he'll just go to sleep, but if they are being honest, they'd be more likely to crash on the sofa. If you know what you are doing and you are happy to sleep with him, then fine, if not say so, but just be true to your own feelings.

5. Of course I love you and respect you

This quote is the saddest one of all. If it is said and meant, then it's wonderful, but if it is said simply to get you to have sex with him, it's very devious. A lot of men and women still approach sex from very different angles – a lot of men are happy to have just physical relationships, where a lot of women demand emotional involvement first. So to speed things up, some boys will just say they love you to get you to have sex. Then, the next day, you won't see them for dust. The only way to avoid this is to use your instincts. If you don't trust him deep down, listen to yourself and don't go any further. You do know when someone really loves and respects you.

6. You would do it if you loved me

Aah, this one is usually said in a wheedling voice and with puppy dog eyes. It's often one of the last resorts, and wheeled out purely to make you feel guilty. If he's not getting anywhere with you he'll pull this one on you and hope that you really feel bad about denying him his love. The thing to do here is to question exactly what his love for you is. Sex does not prove you love someone, and should not be used to do so. If he loves you, he'll want to wait until you both want to have sex, and feel ready to do it. He wouldn't need to convince you by making it into an obligation.

7. It'll make our relationship deeper

Similar to the 'you would if you loved me' statement, this phrase is used to make you feel bad for keeping your relationship back one step, or not proving how much you love him. It's not an untrue statement – sex does change a relationship, but only if the relationship is ready for it and is right in itself. It's not about having sex to prove that you love him a bit more than you said yesterday, it's about having sex because you are both physically and emotionally ready to add this extra dimension to your relationship. Also, sex will not help a relationship that is not working, or make a boy interested in you/ love you if he's not feeling these things already.

8. Everyone else is doing it

Just in case you are incapable of making up your own mind about anything, there's always this old chestnut – designed to make you feel left out of some elite club. And in this case it's the sex club. Even if everyone in your whole town was having sex (highly unlikely), it still shouldn't be a reason to do something yourself if you don't want to. Believe in yourself, and if you start getting pressure of the 'Oh come on, if you don't you'll be the only one who hasn't' kind, tell him where to go.

9. You must be frigid if you don't

It's quite unpleasant when this is said to you, and it's quite an aggressive thing to say when you're meant to be sharing the most wonderful natural experience with the person who's saying it. Of course you won't be 'frigid' if you deny this bloke. It's a word that's mostly only used by boys anyway, and it's not something to spend one minute worrying about. If he does say this to you however, I would worry that he doesn't think very highly of you, as he isn't showing you much respect by calling you names and pressuring you by making you feel paranoid. This would be the last reason on earth why you should actually sleep with someone.

10. I won't tell anyone

Maybe he won't. Hopefully, you both have a mature loving relationship where when you do have sex, you'll both enjoy it, feel closer to each other and then show each other an enormous amount of love and respect. Whether you talk about your experiences is up to you – it's nice to work things through with your best friend if you need to. But if he's saying he'll keep it a secret because there's an element of shame to what you are doing, then be careful. Some boys are about as likely to keep sex a secret as they are to not celebrate if Arsenal won the cup. Bragging about exploits does happen, and if you even slightly worry that he'll make you the brunt of his gossip, you might want to stop right there.

Chapter 12

EMOTIONS Q&A

Wandering hands

I've only been going out with my boyfriend for a few weeks, but he keeps groping me whenever he can. I feel really uncomfortable with it. How can I tell him to slow down?

If this guy has any respect for you he'll calm down once you tell him he makes you feel uncomfortable. His passions are probably just running high because it's the start of a new romance and he really fancies you, but he should be happy to go at your pace. Tell him face to face, in a gentle way – but don't wait for him to start wandering again before you say anything. If he does keep hassling you, then I should cool it off with him until he can show you a lot more respect.

Am I gay?

I can't stop thinking about my best friend. She's really pretty and funny, and we get on so well. But now when I think of her I feel funny inside, and imagine kissing her. I haven't told anyone. Does this mean I am a lesbian, or bisexual? – I have had lots of boy-friends before.

This attraction could mean you are bisexual, a lesbian, or straight. The thing is not to worry about putting labels on yourself this early on in your life. Loads of teenagers fancy people the same sex as them, and then find they change as they get older. Lots of others realise they are gay from an early age. The best thing to do is to focus on getting your own feelings and emotions in perspective. Then when you are really sure, in a few years' time, you'll be able to decide. As to your friend, I wouldn't tell her unless you are one hundred per cent sure that she'd be pleased and return your affection. Value your friendship for now, and see how things work out in the future.

Ex lies

My ex-boyfriend has spread lies round town about me, saying I'm a slag. But we didn't even have sex. Why would he say this and what can I do?

This boy is just trying to punish you for leaving him, and the best way to do this is to make himself look good by talking about your sexual exploits. It's a stupid attitude, so don't even give him the satisfaction of showing that you care. I know you feel let down, but you shouldn't feel humiliated – you've done nothing wrong and should rise above him and all the silly gossips who pander to him. (You could also get your girlfriends to counter the rumour, commenting on how sad he must be to have claimed this when nothing happened between you.)

Should I ask him out?
There's this boy who goes on the bus to school with me who I really fancy. We haven't really spoken, but he keeps staring at me. Should I make the first move?
Well, it's better to talk to him a little before you take the plunge. It sounds like he's interested in you, but the real way to tell if he's keen is to speak to him. Strike up a conversation and if it goes well, and he seems interested, you'll get your first clue. Boys can be very, very shy and really scared about asking a girl out, so don't be afraid to make the first move yourself. What can he do to you other than say no?

Don't worry about feeling silly. If he knocks you back, just shrug it off and make a joke of it, and then maybe you'll get a friendship out of it at least. Good luck.

Will he love me if I have sex?

My boyfriend's pressuring me to sleep with him, and says he'll love me if I do. But I don't know if I believe him.

You are right to feel cautious. Your boyfriend is emotionally blackmailing you into sleeping with him. If he really loves you now, he should tell you that, not make it a condition of sleeping with him. It doesn't sound like he really respects you, so I should wait before you take the next step with him, and if he doesn't open up any more, forget him.

Too drunk

At a party recently I got off with a boy. I was really excited about it the next day, but when I saw him again he said he was too drunk to remember. Could this be true?

Well, he could have been very, very drunk, but I doubt he can't remember a thing. Getting off with someone at a party doesn't mean that you are definitely guaranteed a relationship with him afterwards, unfortunately. It sounds like he's too immature to face you and deal with it. If he doesn't want to go out with you, he should have the decency to tell you honestly, but it doesn't look like he can bring himself to do that. I should cut your losses, and be a bit more selective next time!

Bragging boy

I have been going out with my boyfriend for six months, and I really love him. But lately he's been bragging to all his mates about how far we've gone together. He says he's only joking, but it's really putting me off. What can I do?

It's vital you get him to stop talking about you in this way. Him talking about you shows he doesn't respect you as much as he should, so you need to tell him immediately what you think about all this talk. Try to make him understand why you're upset, and if he can't understand, then I should think twice about your relationship. You deserve better!

Chapter 13

ARE YOU READY FOR SEX?

Are you ready to make the leap into sex? Take the big sex test to discover if your relationship can handle moving to a physical level.

Turn over and follow the flow chart to discover what your type says about you:

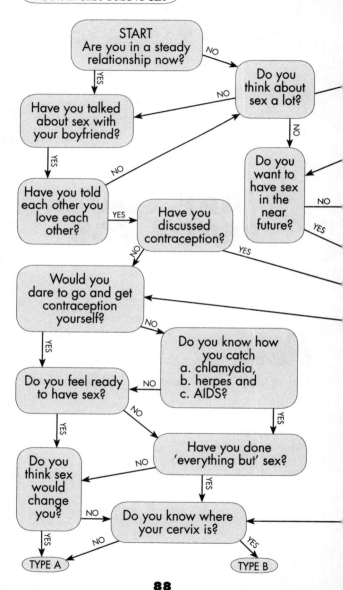

START
Are you in a steady relationship now?

Have you talked about sex with your boyfriend?

Do you think about sex a lot?

Have you told each other you love each other?

Have you discussed contraception?

Do you want to have sex in the near future?

Would you dare to go and get contraception yourself?

Do you know how you catch
a. chlamydia,
b. herpes and
c. AIDS?

Do you feel ready to have sex?

Have you done 'everything but' sex?

Do you think sex would change you?

Do you know where your cervix is?

TYPE A

TYPE B

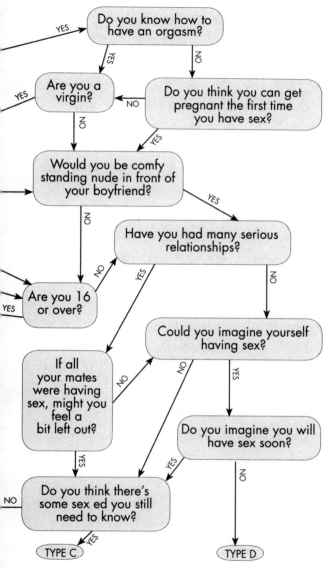

89

Type A - Ready to go . . .

Congratulations! You're a mature young woman who is in a loving and meaningful relationship. You have talked about sex with your boyfriend and have both discussed what you want to get out of a physical relationship. You feel ready emotionally, and believe it will be a pleasurable and enjoyable experience for both of you, and is a step that you are ready to take. You have talked about contraception with your boy-friend, and decided what you will use. You don't feel silly about going to the doctor or clinic to sort your-self out, and want to support each other in that, too.

If all of the above applies to you, then brilliant! If you think some of the areas need improving, make sure you spend time working out exactly what you want emotionally, and always kit yourself out with contraception.

Type B - Fact finder

You are emotionally ready to have sex. You are in a steady relationship, and you have thought about it long and hard. You have talked about it with your boyfriend, too. All of these factors are great, but there is a big BUT. You have some large gaps in your sex knowledge that you need to suss out before you go any further. Make sure you devour the whole of this section, particularly the chapters on STIs (Sexually Transmitted Infections) and contraception, and that you could sit a GCSE in Sex Ed by the end of it! You can never know too much about sex – even some of the brightest girls in the world have made mistakes in the heat of the moment – and that can have serious repercussions through the rest of your life. So get clued-up and save yourself some hassle!

Type C – Maybe later

You are not quite ready to have sex yet. You may be in a long-term relationship, or you may have had a few flings, but having sex is not top of your priority list yet. And even if it was, you need to get yourself clued-up a lot more before you even think about it. You have some serious gaps in your sex knowledge – from what goes where and what bits do what, to what contraception you should use and what STIs you need to know about. The best thing for you to do would be to keep your relationship at the same level you are on now for a little while longer. You'll feel a lot more comfortable that way. Don't pressure yourself into anything, and don't listen to anyone else if they try to persuade you otherwise.

Type D – Stop right there!

You are not ready to have sex at all, but you knew that already, didn't you? You may not even have a boyfriend, or you may not spend much time thinking about sex anyway. You have loads of things going on in your life, and at the moment sex is not important. That's fine – as long as you recognise that, you can give yourself a breather and get on with living your life, until you feel really ready to make such a big leap. In the meantime, make sure you have all the lingo and facts at your fingertips. The good news is, that's what this book's for, and once you've ploughed your way through this whole epic, you'll be able to talk at length about sex education, and think at length about what sex will mean to you. Give yourself a break, and don't worry about it for a while longer.

Chapter 14

VIRGINITY

Virginity. It's one word that is loaded with meaning. Losing it can be a very big deal – it can be a wonderful moment in your life, or it can be a catastrophe. And afterwards, do you feel any different? Do you miraculously turn into a mature young woman? No. But you may be left wondering whether you made the right decision giving it up.

No one else can make your mind up for you about whether you are really ready to lose your virginity. But this chapter could help.

If you really believe you have given the matter a lot of thought and you're ready to lose your virginity, then make sure you have safe sex. Always use a condom to protect against STIs and pregnancy.

Making up your mind

Losing your virginity has to be something *you* want to do. You have to be ready to take this step, and be aware of all the extra levels that a sexual relationship will add to your relationship. It's about deciding what your own set of sexual guidelines are going to be. You have to be happy with the decisions you make in your sex life – like who you sleep with, how many partners you have, making up your mind whether to have a sexual relationship with someone new. As long as you are happy with those decisions, and you have no regrets about decisions you have made, then you will be doing the right thing, for you.

Waiting to have sex

Some people decide that they want to wait until they are married before they have sex. This is their choice, and a decision that means a lot to them. It may be for moral reasons, or religious beliefs, and is one that should be respected by anyone else.

Memories

You will probably have a lot of sex in your life, and maybe a few partners. But the first time will stay in your memory for ever. Whatever it's like, you will never forget. So do yourself a favour and make it as good as you can, so you look back fondly, not with regret. Make sure you honestly think he's the right one, and you are sure he's the one you want to take your virginity, not just the person of the moment.

Be prepared

If you are going to lose your virginity, the best thing you can do for yourself is to make it good. Prepare where and when you are going to do it, and make it an experience that you will be happy to keep as a memory for the rest of your life. Make sure you have discussed what you expect, with your partner, and you are both able to make it special for each other. Above all, get contraception that covers both STIs and pregnancy.

Sex – the truth

Although you should do all of the above, don't expect too much from your first time! There may not be romance and fireworks, and it won't be like in the movies. Sex is intimate, messy and embarrassing. You and he may fumble putting the condom on, it may hurt a little, and you won't necessarily have an orgasm! It could even be over in six seconds flat. Don't pressure yourself with expectations, but just go with the flow.

No regrets

If you *do* regret losing your virginity, you don't have to beat yourself up about it. You can't get it back, that's true, but you don't have to keep having sex just because you have done it once. If you were not happy with your decision, then put your sex life on hold, and don't worry about it for a while. You don't have to continue having sex with the same person, and you don't have to rush into sexual relationships with anyone else if you don't want to. Remember that you are always in control of your own destiny.

Chapter 15

CONTRACEPTION

The best way to arm yourself against pregnancy and Sexually Transmitted Infections is to know all the facts about contraception. So here's the definitive guide to contraception today.

Condom
What it is: A thin latex sheath that covers a boy's penis.
How it works: It catches the sperm rather than let it go inside you.
How effective: 85–98% effective.
Advantages: It's free from family planning clinics and can be bought in any chemist or pub toilet.
Disadvantages: It can slip off or tear if not used properly.

Comments: Use a new condom each time you have sex. Make sure it has a British Kitemark or European CE mark on it and check the expiry date.

Does it protect against STIs? YES

Female condom

What it is: A thin polyurethane sleeve that fits into the vagina.

How it works: It blocks the sperm from going into your cervix.

How effective: 85–98% effective.

Advantages: It can be put in any time before sex.

Disadvantages: It can be tricky to use and is expensive.

Comments: You need a new one each time you have sex.

Does it protect against STIs? YES

The pill

There are two types of contraceptive pill – the combined pill and progestogen-only pill. Your doctor will advise which is best for you.

The combined pill

What it is: It's a pill which contains a mixture of the hormones oestrogen and progestogen and is taken every day.

How it works: It stops you producing an egg each month.

How effective: Almost 100%.

Advantages: It reduces bleeding, period pain and PMS. It can also protect against cancer in the ovary or womb.

Disadvantages: You can get some side-effects like headaches and feeling sick, bloating and weight gain.

Comments: It's not suitable for everyone – your doctor will advise.

Does it protect against STIs? NO

The progestogen-only pill

What it is: It's a pill containing the hormone progestogen and is taken every day.

How it works: It thickens cervical mucus, so it makes it hard for the sperm to swim up the Fallopian tubes. Plus it thins the womb lining, making it inhospitable for a fertilised egg.

How effective: 96–99%.

Advantages: It's good for women who can't take the combined pill.

Disadvantages: Periods may become irregular, with some bleeding in between.

Comments: You must not forget to take this pill at the same time every day.

Does it protect against STIs? NO

Diaphragm or Cap

What it is: It's a soft rubber disk or bowl that fits at the top of your vagina and covers your cervix.

How it works: Used with spermicide, it stops sperm entering your cervix.

How effective: 85–96%.

Advantages: It can be put in a few hours before sex.

Disadvantages: If you have sex again, you need to use more spermicide. It can be tricky to learn how to use the cap, and you have to leave it in for hours after you have had sex.

Comments: You have to get it fitted by your doctor.

Does it protect against STIs? NO

Contraceptive injection

What it is: *Depo Provera* is an injection of the hormone progestogen.

How it works: It disrupts your production of eggs and your menstrual cycle.

How effective: 99%.

Advantages: You don't have to worry about contraception once you have had it, for twelve weeks.

Disadvantages: You can get some side-effects like irregular periods and weight gain.

Comments: Once you've had one, you can't stop it until it runs out.

Does it protect against STIs? NO

Contraceptive implant

What it is: It's six hormone capsules which are surgically inserted into your arm.

How it works: The hormones are time-released and stop you ovulating. It also thickens the mucus in your cervix, helping to stop sperm reaching the egg.

How effective: 99%.

Advantages: It works for 5 years, so you needn't worry about contraception.

Disadvantages: It's hard to have it removed if you change your mind. It can also cause periods to become irregular and you can get side-effects like greasy hair and acne.

Comments: Once it's in, you can't see it.

Does it protect against STIs? NO

The IUS

What it is: This is the Intra Uterine System. It's a small, T-shaped plastic device which contains the hormone progestogen. It is fitted into your womb by a doctor.

How it works: It slowly releases the hormone progestogen, which thickens the mucus in your cervix, helping to stop sperm reaching an egg, and it thins the womb lining, making it inhospitable to an egg.

How effective: Almost 100%.

Advantages: It works for at least three years and periods can get shorter and lighter.

Disadvantages: You might get irregular bleeding and have side-effects like tender boobs and acne.

Comments: You feel it's in place by some light threads which hang into your vagina.

Does it protect against STIs? NO

The IUD
What it is: Similar to the IUS, this is the Intra Uterine Device. It's a small plastic and copper device, usually shaped like a 'T', that is fitted into the uterus by a doctor.

How it works: It works by stopping sperm meeting an egg, or by stopping an egg settling in the womb.

How effective: 98–99%.

Advantages: It works for five years.

Disadvantages: You may get heavier and more painful periods.

Comments: It is unsuitable for women who have more than one sexual partner. It's not often given to young women.

Does it protect against STIs? NO

All information taken from the Family Planning Clinic's leaflet 'Is Everybody Doing It? Your Guide to Contraception'.

Chapter 16

SEXUALLY TRANSMITTED INFECTIONS

Unfortunately, in today's world, as well as contraception you need to know about all the diseases you are at risk of catching if you don't have safe sex. So do yourself a favour and protect yourself with knowledge.

Chlamydia
What it is: Currently one of the most common sexually transmitted infections in the UK. Women aged 16–19 are most at risk. If not treated it can lead to infertility.

How you get it: Chlamydia is passed through vaginal sex, or by transferring the infection from his or your genitals to the eyes by touching genitals and then touching the eyes.

Know it: The problem is, most women don't get any symptoms. However, you should watch out for: a mild increase in vaginal discharge, the need to wee more often and painful weeing, tummy ache and irregular bleeding, pain during sex, swelling or irritation of the eyes. Men should look out for: white/cloudy discharge from the penis, the need to wee more often, painful weeing, and swelling or irritation of the eyes.

Cure: Antibiotics.

Genital herpes

What it is: Genital herpes is caused by the herpes simplex virus. There are two different types of this virus: type I causes sores on the nose and mouth and type II causes sores in the genital and anal area. New cases of genital herpes are most common among 20–24-year-olds.

How you get it: It's passed through direct contact with an infected person, through kissing, oral sex, penetrative sex or anal sex. You can catch herpes from someone who may have no signs of it at all.

Know it: You'll get an itching or tingling sensation around the mouth or genital/anal area. Small

105

THE SMART GIRL'S GUIDE TO **SEX**

blisters then develop, which burst and leave painful sores. You might also get flu-like symptoms. During this period the virus is highly infectious and so all sexual contact should be avoided.

Cure: NONE. Once you catch it, you can't cure it – but you have to learn to live with it. Attacks can reoccur at any time.

Genital warts

What it is: They are small fleshy growths, like tiny cauliflowers, that grow on or around the genital area/anus. Women aged 16–19 are currently the category with the highest rate of infection, as well as men aged 20–24.

How you get it: Genital warts are transmitted through skin to skin contact of the genitals, including vaginal, anal and oral sex.

Know it: Some strains of the virus can be almost invisible, or cause no warts at all, others look like the description above. They can appear alone or in clusters. They may itch, but usually they are painless. In women, warts can develop inside the vagina and on the cervix (which can sometimes cause bleeding).

Cure: A paint-on solution called Podophyllin is

often used in the treatment of genital warts, or they could be frozen off or laser treated.

Gonorrhoea

What it is: Gonorrhoea is a sexually transmitted infection which is also known as 'the clap'. The infection has been around for thousands of years, and is even mentioned in the *Bible*. It was once thought to be dying out, but it's on the increase again, and teenagers are one of the highest risk categories.

How you get it: It's a bacterial infection caught through vaginal, anal or oral sex.

Know it: Women may not show any symptoms. But men should watch out for the penis producing a thick, runny discharge. Discharge or irritation may also occur from the anus. Weeing may become painful, and a sore throat can develop. If left untreated, a rash can develop that can affect the nervous system.

Cure: Penicillin.

Pubic lice

What it is: Pubic lice are also known as 'crabs'. They are tiny grey insects, about the size of a full stop, that can attach themselves to pubic hair, armpit hair and sometimes the eyebrows.

How you get it: Pubic lice are generally transmitted through intimate contact with someone who has them. However, they can also be picked up from bedding, clothes and towels used by an infected person.

Know it: Pubic lice are often mistaken for loose flakes of skin in the genital area, but unlike skin, however, they move and may itch.

Cure: Your doctor will prescribe highly effective lotions.

HIV and AIDS

What it is: HIV stands for Human Immunodeficiency Virus. Someone who has the virus is said to be HIV Positive. HIV attacks the body's immune system. People with HIV usually stay well for many years before they develop AIDS itself. AIDS stands for Acquired Immune Deficiency Syndrome. It is a collection of illnesses and conditions that arise as the body's immune system is weakened by HIV infection.

How you get it: HIV is transmitted through unprotected sex, including anal sex. The virus can't

survive outside the body, but is passed through
bodily fluids like semen or vaginal secretions. This
means that unprotected oral sex is a risk if there
are cuts or lesions present. It can also be passed
through blood, such as sharing needles for intrave-
nous drug use.

Know it: HIV symptoms are: night sweats, fever,
lack of energy, diarrhoea and weight-loss, thrush
or herpes infections, dry skin and rashes, mouth
ulcers and bleeding gums. AIDS-related symptoms
which can then develop are: breathing problems,
eyesight difficulties and infections, brain problems
and cancer.

Cure: NONE.

Hepatitis

What it is: Hepatitis is a viral infection of
the liver. There are two types – hepatitis A and
hepatitis B.

How you get it: Hepatitis A is an infection
that is mainly spread through poor hygiene, poo
and contaminated food. It's not really a sexually
transmitted infection. However, hepatitis B is much
more infectious than HIV and can be transmitted
through sexual contact, and contact with blood or

saliva containing blood traces. You should also beware of dirty tools used in body piercing and tattooing.

Know it: Symptoms are: lack of energy and appetite, fever, jaundiced (yellow) skin, yellowing whites of eyes, pale poo and dark wee and abdominal pain.

Cure: NONE. But people do recover after rest and healthy living.

Be aware that many sexually transmitted diseases do not produce physical symptoms for months, which means you risk infecting others through unprotected sexual intercourse. Be safe. *Always* use a condom.

FEMALE HEALTH

There are some other infections that are not sexually transmitted, but are very common. In case you develop one, learn to recognise them and their cures.

Cystitis

This is a common infection and/or inflammation of the bladder lining, which makes it searingly painful to wee, and makes you think you have to wee all the time. Cystitis is caused by anal or vaginal bacteria reaching the urethra (often as a result of sex or through not drinking enough fluid to flush germs from the bladder). Wearing tight trousers or underwear can also create a warm environment for bacteria to breed.

Sort it: Drink half a litre of water straight away (some people recommend cranberry juice as an effective alternative) and then a quarter of a litre every twenty minutes until you are going to the toilet without any problems. Don't resist the urge to pee, even if it hurts, as any urine passed will help to flush out the infection. You can also buy special formulas from the chemist to help.

Thrush

This is an uncomfortable condition caused by an imbalance in a naturally occurring yeast-like fungus (*Candida albicans*) that lives on the skin and mouth and inside the vagina. Normally levels are kept under control by the presence of certain bacteria, but these can be disturbed by stress, taking antibiotics, wearing tight-fitting clothes and sex with someone who has thrush. Symptoms include vaginal soreness and inflammation and/or pain when passing urine.

You may also notice an increase in discharge, which has changed colour, smells and itches.

Sort it: Thrush can be easily treated with over-the-counter creams like Canestan or a pessary (a small tablet inserted inside the vagina with a special applicator) both of which are available from chemists. Applying natural live yoghurt can also relieve the discomfort, while sex should be avoided until the symptoms have cleared.

Vaginismus

This is a strong, involuntary tightening or spasm of the vaginal muscles, making sex painful or impossible. The cause of vaginismus is thought to be psychological, often due to previous sexual trauma or anxieties relating to intercourse.

Sort it: Take sex off the agenda and focus instead on intimacy with your partner. Basically, whatever you feel comfortable doing. If the situation doesn't improve, ask your doctor to refer you to a trained counsellor who can help you identify the cause of the problem and help you overcome it.

All statistics taken from theSite by YouthNet, at www.thesite.org.

Chapter 17

SEX – EVERYTHING YOU EVER WANTED TO KNOW BUT DAREN'T ASK

When it comes to having sex, you won't be alone in wondering how you actually do it. Well, surprise surprise, there's no magic answer or step-by-step guide to making love, but there are some answers to all those niggling questions you've ever wanted to ask.

How do you actually have sex?

Sex is technically when a boy puts his penis inside a girl's vagina, and then moves it in and out rhythmically, until he, or both of them have an orgasm. That's it!

Are there special positions in which to have sex?

No, there's no magic position you should memorise, it's more a case of finding out what feels nice as you go along. However, there are some main positions in which people often have sex:

Missionary This is the traditional sex position, and involves the boy lying on top of the girl.

Doggy style This is where the girl kneels on all fours, and the boy kneels behind her.

Girl on top The girl sits on top of the boy, who is lying down.

Standing up This can be tricky, and is easier if you lean against a wall.

Sitting down This is usually done with the boy sitting on a chair, and the girl straddling him, facing him or facing away.

Side by side Otherwise known as 'spoons', the girl lies on her side, with the boy behind her.

What's a 69?

This is a sexual position that is probably talked about more than actually done! It is where the boy and girl give each other oral sex at the same time, by lying down with their heads at opposite ends of each other.

And what's anal sex?

Anal sex is what it says – it's when a boy has sex in your anus, or bum-hole, rather than your vagina. Some people enjoy it, some find it painful or dirty. It's up to you. Remember you should always use a condom if you do this, as STIs including HIV can be spread this way.

What exactly is a blowjob?

This is when a girl gives a boy oral sex. It actually has nothing to do with blowing, as blowing down the end of a penis could be dangerous. It's simply where a girl uses her mouth and tongue to excite a boy – by licking and sucking his penis. Make sure you don't catch his penis with your teeth, but apart from that, just see what feels nice for both of you at the time.

And do you swallow sperm?

If you are giving a boy oral sex and he wants to have an orgasm, you can swallow his semen, or spit it out. Sperm tastes tangy but won't do you any harm (and no, you can't get pregnant by swallowing it). If you do not want to swallow, you can take your mouth away before he orgasms, and either use your hand to catch it or use a tissue.

Do you have to orgasm every time you have sex?

No – but it would be nice! A girl doesn't always orgasm in sex, some women never do, some do all the time.

What is foreplay?

Foreplay is the term used for all the intimate acts you do in the lead-up to sex – caressing, kissing, oral sex, etc. Foreplay is often seen as more important for women, as it arouses you gradually and makes you ready for sex – whereas men are often ready for sex instantly, when they are aroused and get an erection. However most partners should get pleasure from foreplay.

And what's the difference between that and heavy petting?

Heavy petting is a bit of a granny-saying for when you are 'getting it on' with someone. The difference is foreplay is going to lead to sex, heavy petting is an end in itself and doesn't necessarily lead to sex.

Can you have sex during your period?

Yes, you can – if you want to. Many people do, though many others find it messy and horrible. It's up to you! It's safe as in it won't harm you, but it will make a mess, so use a towel or something beneath you, and always use contraception, as you can still get pregnant during your period.

How long is sex meant to take?

Thirteen and a half minutes. No, I'm joking! It can take as long or as short as you want. Sometimes it's over in minutes, sometimes it takes hours. As long as you are enjoying it, there's no set time limit. And remember – sex isn't just penetrative sex, it's all the other things you do too.

Are you meant to talk during sex?

Again, if you want to. It's up to you. Some people find talking dirty turns them on, some people simply chat during sex, or joke, or talk about what they are doing – is the other person enjoying it, would they like to do something else or do something differently, and the same for what you'd like. Some people remain absolutely silent and find talking embarrassing. It's a case of doing what comes naturally to you and your partner.

117

Are you meant to make any noise?

You don't have to make moans and groans like in the movies. Again, it's up to you. Some people shriek without knowing what they are doing, others make a few little squeaks of pleasure. You can do what you like.

How do lesbians have sex?

Lesbians have sex the same way heterosexuals do – they just don't do the penetration bit. They kiss and cuddle and use their mouths, hands and tongues to give each other pleasure.

How do I know if he has had an orgasm?

When a boy orgasms he'll feel a release of tension and sort of shudder. He will also ejaculate semen, which is a clear sign he has 'come'.

And me?

Women don't ejaculate, so you can't tell if they have had an orgasm as obviously as you can with boys. Your body will become tense and you'll sort of shiver as you orgasm, and you'll experience a rush of feeling inside you. Women can have multiple orgasms, where wave upon wave of feeling will hit them. It sounds hard to identify, but if you have an orgasm, you know it!

What happens if I make a mistake?

Sex is not a deadly serious act, to be studied and worried about. Sex is fun, and there's no right and wrong way to do it. If you are messing around with your boyfriend and you do something clumsy, or make a funny noise, just laugh it off. It's far, far different to sex you see on TV – all moonlight and soft focus camera angles. Real sex is messy, funny and silly. You might do all sorts of things in the middle of it – from farting or burping, to your tummy roaring, your bodies rubbing together and making a farty sound or – as sometimes happens during sex – you might get air expelling from your vagina in a 'fanny fart'. If anything funny happens to you, just laugh – you should be close enough to your boyfriend to find these sorts of mishaps funny rather than mortifying. If he doesn't let it go without making you feel stupid, then you should ask some serious questions as to why you are having sex with him in the first place. Just don't worry!

Chapter 18

SEX MYTHS
– BUSTED

We girls have to plough our way through a lot of nonsense in the world of sex. From nasty rumours to old wives' tales, it's best to be prepared. So here's your guide to the top ten tall tales told about sex.

1. You can't get pregnant the first time you have sex.

This is rubbish. Of course you can. If you've started your periods then you are fertile. Each time a boy ejaculates he shoots out six hundred million sperm. It takes just one of them to get you pregnant. Plus, even if you haven't started your periods, it's still unsafe to have unprotected sex, as you never know when you will start.

2. You can't get pregnant during your period.

This is totally untrue. There is a chance that you can get pregnant during a period, particularly towards the end of it. You should always use protection.

3. You can't get pregnant while having sex standing up, or in the shower or bath.

It doesn't matter where you have sex, or what position you have it in, if you have unprotected sex you can get pregnant.

4. Condoms are 100% safe.

Condoms are a highly effective form of contraception, as well as a great way of preventing STIs. However, condoms can and do break, so it's always better to use them in conjunction with another form of contraception such as the pill.

5. You can't get pregnant while on the pill.

This is fairly true – the chances of getting pregnant while taking the contraceptive pill are virtually nil, providing you follow the instructions correctly and consistently. However, if you miss one, or take one at the wrong time (depending on the type of pill you use) you could be at risk. Read the instructions carefully and if you are in doubt, go back to your doctor. Also, if you have sickness or diarrhoea it can affect the pill and it may not work as effectively, so if you have had these, always use a condom as well.

6. If a condom breaks, there's nothing you can do.

Yes there is. You can get emergency contraception. You must go and see your doctor immediately, and he/she will prescribe you the morning-after pill, which can be taken up to seventy-two hours after having unprotected sex. They can also fit a coil (IUD) as emergency contraception, which works up to five days after having unprotected sex.

7. All boys hate using condoms.

The only guys who don't like using condoms are those with no respect for you. Don't listen to anyone that says sex doesn't feel nice wearing a condom, either. Obviously you don't get skin-to-skin contact, and the boy loses a tiny bit of sensation, but it doesn't make that much difference – and it's just not worth the risk to not use one. It's best not to rely on a lad to provide condoms. If you're considering sex then take responsibility for yourself.

8. If you douche with something like cola after sex, it'll stop you getting pregnant.

Goodness knows where this myth came from, but it is a myth and it's wrong. Douching with water and soap can be dangerous as it can upset your vagina's natural balance and cause irritation. Douching with cola is unthinkable. It'll cause you some discomfort, and it won't stop you getting pregnant.

9. You can't get the pill if you're under sixteen.

This is a contentious issue. You can get the pill from your doctor if they believe that you are going to have sex anyway, whether they give you contraception or not, even though it's illegal for you to have sex under-age. They do not have to tell your parents that you have seen them, either.

10. Everyone's at it.

This last myth is important, because although it may seem silly, it's something that appears to be true. You see so much guff about sex on TV, in films, in the papers, and all your mates seem to be sniggering about sex stories they're telling. Sometimes, the whole thing makes you feel well left out. Just remember – more people talk about it than actually do it, and the ones that are talking the loudest, are usually the ones that are doing it the least.

Chapter 19

SEX – WHEN YOU DON'T WANT IT

Sex can be a wonderful expression of love between two people. Unfortunately it can also be an act of aggression, when it's forced on you when you don't want it. This chapter's about the times when sex turns bad.

SEXUAL HARASSMENT

Sexual harassment can take many forms – from persistent sexual comments at work or school which upset and affect you, right through to being touched or groped by someone.

Verbal
Different people have different levels of tolerance for 'sexy' talk. Some women just laugh it off and answer

back and see it as a bit of banter in the workplace or at school. Others feel really uncomfortable with it and find it affecting them deeply.

If you are in this situation, work out your own reaction to it. If it doesn't bother you, then fine, the men saying things probably just think they are having a laugh anyway. If it does bother you, then calmly and politely mention it to the people involved and say it makes you uncomfortable. If they don't stop, tell someone in authority.

Physical

No woman should have to put up with being touched or groped by anyone. It's often done by people in positions of power, as they bank on the other person feeling that they'd either lose their job or that no one would believe them. If it happens to you, calmly talk to this person about their actions and insist they stop. If they don't, report them to someone in authority. If that doesn't work, you *can* sue.

RAPE

Although rape is about sex, it is also an act of power and aggression. If anyone forces another person to have sex against their will, then that is rape. It's illegal and the maximum penalty is life imprisonment.

Sadly many rapes are never reported to the police because of the shame and feelings of guilt that are wrongly felt by the victims.

Technically, rape is forced sexual intercourse. If someone touches you intimately or makes you perform other sex acts with them, then that is classed as sexual assault.

Protect yourself

Rape is a terrible ordeal to go through. Protect yourself by following these tips:

• Whenever you can, walk with a group of people.

• Know where you are going and act like it. Walk with your head high and a purposeful stride. If you are walking a long way, wear shoes you can walk fast or run in.

• Don't walk down dark alleyways or remote roads on your own.

• Follow your instincts. If you feel uncomfortable in an area or situation, leave, or run, immediately.

• If you are catching a cab, never get in an unmarked minicab – there are people who pretend to be cab drivers. If you do catch a minicab, get in and out with a friend.

- Carry a rape alarm and take self-defence classes.
- Choose the busiest train carriages, and sit near the bus driver.
- Don't accept lifts from strangers, ever.

What to do

If you are raped, there are some important things you should remember:

- It is not your fault. Never feel guilty. No woman deserves to be raped, and there's no such thing as 'asking for it'. It doesn't matter what you are wearing or doing.
- Report it to the police immediately. Don't be worried – they have specially trained police doctors and officers who will reassure you.
- Do not wash yourself or your clothes and don't throw anything away – even if you feel really dirty. Your body and clothes will provide important DNA clues to the identity of the rapist.
- Get counselling. The police will offer you some counsellors to help you get through your trauma. Talking about it will help you get over it.
- Get yourself emergency contraception, and later, have an STI and HIV test.

Date rape

Most rapes are committed by someone the victim knows. This has led to a new type of rape being legally defined – date rape.

There are many date rape scenarios, from a first date, to rape by a 'friend', or at the start of a relationship. Alcohol often plays a big role – where people get drunk, start messing around, she says no, and he won't stop.

The best way to avoid situations like these is to make sure you never end up getting intimate with someone you don't completely trust. If you're with a man and he starts displaying aggressive or erratic behaviour, get out. And don't let yourself get so drunk or high that you don't know what you are doing.

Date Rape Drug

The date rape drug, Rohypnol, is a powerful sedative, ten times stronger than Valium. Rapists have been known to slip it into a girl's drink, at a party or pub or club. The woman then becomes really dizzy and may black out, and the rapist carries her out as if she were drunk. Many women wake up and have no recollection that they have been raped.

Never accept a drink from someone you don't feel safe with.

SEXUAL ABUSE

Sexual abuse is when someone in a position of authority (from inside or outside the home) takes advantage of your trust in them to have sex with you.

Being the ongoing victim of sexual abuse can have serious long-term effects on your life. Victims may find themselves suffering from depression, eating disorders, drink or drug addictions and have trouble having relationships themselves, later in their lives.

Anyone who ever experiences sexual abuse must tell someone straight away. Many cases go on so long because the victim is afraid tell anyone. If it should happen to you, remember that it is *not* your fault and it is wrong for this person to do this to you. It doesn't matter if you love them or they love you, they are abusing you and must be stopped. It is not something anyone should put up with – and the only way to stop this is to tell someone you trust – a parent, teacher, friend, or friend's parent. Only then will you be able to get help, and start rebuilding your life. If you've no one you feel you can turn to then phone the NSPCC on 0800 800 500 or Childline on 0800 1111.

Chapter 20

GETTING PREGNANT

Britain has the highest rate of teenage pregnancies in Western Europe. Thousands of girls discover they are pregnant each year, and then face a really tough decision – what to do. In the *Bliss* Sex and Teen Mums Survey 1998, seventy-five per cent of you said you knew someone who got pregnant as a teenager. So *always* use contraception and safeguard yourself from ever having to make these decisions.

If you discover you're pregnant you will have to face three clear choices:
1. Keep the baby,
2. Have the baby adopted,
3. Have an abortion.

No choice may be completely right, and making your decision will be the hardest thing you've had to do in your life so far. This chapter will not make up your mind for you, but will help you understand your choices.

Firstly, you must tell someone, and get advice from your boyfriend, parents, good friends and your doctor. It's too hard a decision to make on your own. You may be scared of telling your parents and, yes, they are not going to be thrilled by your news. But your parents do love you, and most of them are surprisingly resilient creatures and will do everything they can to help you, after they've recovered from the shock.

The worst thing you could do is to ignore it, and hope it goes away. It won't.

Here are your options:

1. Keep the baby

It's important you understand that nothing will change your life as much as having a baby. Things you take for granted now – like taking your exams, going to university, getting a career, and going out with your mates and having a laugh, will be difficult and maybe impossible with a baby. You need to prepare yourself:

• Where will you live?

• How will you manage financially?
• Will you stay in school?
• Can you cope with a child for the next eighteen years?
• If you decide to go through with it, you will need to go to your doctor and start your antenatal care immediately.

2. Adoption

Giving up a baby for adoption is not easy – for the mother or father. It is best to talk to someone about this as soon as possible, such as your doctor or someone at the antenatal clinic.

The adoption will probably be handled by a social worker who will discuss the kind of family the birth parents want their child to grow up in, and will try to find out as much as possible about the birth family to pass on to the adopters.

When the child has settled down with the new family, the adoptive parents will apply to the court for an adoption order, which will be granted if the court is satisfied that all is well.

Neither birth parent has the right to see their child after she or he has been adopted, although the child can get in touch with them after the age of eighteen.

Help and advice for anyone thinking of having their child adopted is available through the British Agencies for Adoption and Fostering.

3. Abortion

Abortion is a personal issue, based on what feels right for the individual involved. It is an extremely difficult choice, and no one should push you into making the decision.

If you really believe that you can't go through with the pregnancy, it will help to talk to someone about it beforehand. Again, talk to a trusted friend and parent. Then see your doctor immediately, as abortions must be performed in the early stages of pregnancy.

Abortion in England, Scotland or Wales is legal as long as it follows the law set out in the Abortion Act, 1967. This states that an abortion may be legally carried out if:

• Two doctors agree that continuing the pregnancy would risk the life of the mother or risk injury to her physical or mental health. Concern over the mother's mental health is a common reason for doctors to allow an abortion, particularly if they feel she is likely to suffer excessive emotional strain.

• Two doctors agree that there is a substantial risk

that the child might be born seriously physically or mentally handicapped.

An abortion must by law, except in a few extreme cases, be carried out before the twenty-fourth week of pregnancy. If you want the abortion on the National Health you'll need to start making the arrangements before the twelfth week.

If you are under sixteen, your parents must give their consent to end the pregnancy, unless two doctors decide that you are mature enough to understand what their decision really means. But doctors normally insist on having a parent's consent before giving you a general anaesthetic.

An abortion can be given without anaesthetic, through tablets. But these are normally used only within the first eight weeks of a pregnancy.

The father, whether married to the girl or not, has no right to prevent her from having a legal abortion.

A doctor does not have to carry out an abortion if it is against his or her conscience. If that happens, see another doctor.

This information is provided by the Citizenship Foundation.

Chapter 21

SEX Q&A

Condom split

When I had sex with my boyfriend, the condom split and a bit of it was left inside me. I got it out, but could I be pregnant?

Yes, you could. After a boy 'comes', he should hold the condom firmly against his penis as he withdraws. If the condom stays inside, or splits, sperm can then swim up your vagina and this could lead to pregnancy. You must get yourself emergency contraception now – go and see your doctor and get the morning-after pill, which can be taken up to seventy-two hours after sex.

Sex pest

My dad's friend keeps popping round to see me

when Dad isn't there. He keeps groping me and making suggestive comments. What can I do?

You need to tell your mum and dad at once. This man is acting very dangerously and must be stopped. He's taking advantage of you because he's a family friend and thinks you won't tell, so you should stop him now before he goes any further.

Period query

I want to know if you can have sex before your periods start. If so, do you have to use contraception?

Your periods start after you have gone through puberty. Puberty gives you all the outward signs of turning into a woman, but also changes you internally – your womb gets bigger and your vagina lengthens and widens to accommodate a penis. So if you haven't gone through puberty and started your periods, then no, it is not advisable to have sex.

However, if you did, you'd have to use contraception, as you can never tell when your periods are going to start, and you may be fertile without knowing it.

Doctor fear

I want to get contraception, but I'm worried about

seeing my doctor as he's a family friend. Would he tell my parents?

No, he could not tell your parents as he has to keep all patients' files confidential. He would keep his professional relationship separate from his personal friendship with you and your parents, so don't be embarrassed to see him. But if you don't want to go to him, you can go to a Brook Advisory Centre or a family planning clinic, both of which offer specialised contraception services. Look in your phone book for your nearest branch.

Itchy bits
My boyfriend's penis itches all the time. What could be wrong with him?

An itchy penis, or vaginal area, could be a sign of an STI. Left untreated this could cause serious problems for you and your boyfriend. Go to your doctor or clinic immediately and get yourselves checked out.

Missed a date
I think I have missed a period. I have irregular periods anyway, but this one is really late. I had sex, but we used a condom. Could I be pregnant?

You could be pregnant if you didn't use the condom

correctly and some of the sperm entered your vagina – or if your boyfriend put his penis inside you before he put the condom on, as some sperm can leak out before he orgasms.

Having irregular periods doesn't make it less likely you'll conceive, but can make it confusing. You must go to your doctor straight away, and have a pregnancy test.

Virgin worry

My boyfriend and I are both virgins. We're thinking about having sex. Do you have to worry about STIs if you are a virgin?

STIs are usually transmitted through sexual intercourse, but there are some that can be passed through kissing or other sex acts, like oral sex. So there is still a risk of infection if you have done this with anyone else. If there is any discharge, inflammation or sores around you or your boyfriend's genitals, you should go to a clinic. Even if there isn't, you should still use condoms to protect against STIs and pregnancy.

Did I have sex?

I was messing about with my boyfriend and he started asking me to have sex. I don't want to quite

yet, but as we were getting it together, he put his penis inside me for a little while. Does this mean I have had sex – and am I still a virgin?

Technically, you lose your virginity when a boy's penis enters your vagina, but most people class losing their virginity as when they actually have sex – i.e. when a boy puts his penis inside a girl's vagina and moves it in and out repetitively until he ejaculates.

There are two issues: One is that I hope you used contraception. The other is that you didn't want to have sex, but your boyfriend went further anyway. Make sure you talk to him long and hard about what you do and don't feel comfortable with. Your first time should be special, and he should respect that.

Withdrawal worry

My boyfriend says if he pulls out his willy before he orgasms, he doesn't need a condom. Is this true?

No, it's not true. There are two problems with this. One is that it's highly likely that at some point he won't be able to withdraw fast enough and may leave some semen inside you, or right near your vagina. The second is that even before a boy orgasms he leaks some sperm. So you should always use contraception.

RESOURCES

For further help or information contact:

Contraception & Pregnancy

Brook Advisory Centres

Will help arrange contraception and offer advice on a wide range of sex issues. Especially helpful for young people.

For your nearest branch, call 0800 018 5023 Mon, Tues and Thurs 9a.m.–5p.m., Weds and Fri, 9a.m.–4p.m. *Bliss* and Brook Advisory Centres have got together to give you specially recorded information on helplines that run 24 hours a day, 7 days a week. All calls are charged at the normal rate for a call to London:
Guide to contraception: 020 7285 5510
Had unprotected sex?: 020 7285 5511
Missed your period?: 020 7285 5512
All about abortion: 020 7285 5513
Pregnant and confused: 020 7285 5514
Going to a Brook Centre: 020 7285 5515

The Family Planning Association

Runs clinics for anything to do with sexual health:
FPA UK: 020 7837 4044 (9a.m.–7p.m.)
FPA Scotland: 0141 576 5088 (9a.m.–5p.m.)
FPA Wales: 01222 342766 (9a.m.–5p.m.)
FPA Northern Ireland: 01232 325488 (9a.m.–5p.m.)

The British Pregnancy Advisory Service

A referral service for all types of birth control, but also helps with counselling and advice on abortion. For your nearest

clinic call the BPAS Actionline on 08457 30 40 30 or e-mail
them on info@bpas.org or visit www.bpas.demon.co.uk.

British Agencies for Adoption and Fostering:
0207 593 2000

Avert (AIDS Education & Research Trust):
Free information service on HIV, AIDS and related matters:
01403 210202

Sexually Transmitted Infections

For your nearest STI (Sexually Transmitted Infections) or
GUM (Genitourinary Medicine) clinics, check your phone
book. The clinics are usually attached to a hospital.

National AIDS helpline
Confidential advice on HIV and AIDS. Calls are free and
won't show up on your phone bill: 0800 567 123

Problems & Advice

Youth Access: Can refer you to appropriate counselling
service anywhere in the UK, whatever your problem: 020
8772 9900

Lesbian and Gay Switchboard: Provides information
and confidential advice over the phone: 020 7837 7324

The Samaritans: 24-hour help: 0345 909090

Rape Crisis Centre: Confidential counselling: 020 7837 1600

Childline: Free 24-hour helpline for any young person with
a problem: 0800 1111

The British Association for Counselling: Write to:
1 Regent Place, Rugby CV21 2PJ for local counsellors to
help, or call 01788 550899.

Adoption & Fostering Information Line:
Helps those involved in adoption: 0800 783 4086

SPOD: Advice on issues around sex for people with a
disability: 020 7607 8851

Online Help
theSite: Online site for young people about all aspects of
their lives – including great information on sex, STIs and
contraception, and advice chat rooms: www.youthnet.org.uk

SHASTD: Society of Health Advisors in Sexually
Transmitted Diseases. Offers the last word on STIs and covers
any query you may have on the topic: www.shastd.org.uk

Teen Advice: An American site, but offers a good advice
service and has a large base of archived problems and
articles: www.teenadviceonline.org

Teen wire: A site by the Planned Parenthood Federation of
America. Huge warehouse of articles on issues to do with
love and sex, advice and quizzes: www.teenwire.com

NHS: For all health issues: www.nhsdirect.nhs.uk

Lovelife: A good site for young people covering all areas of
sex and love. It's from the Health Education Authority:
www.lovelife.hea.org.uk

INDEX